MOM  3MD

A Mother's Story

A Memoir by

Rose A. Hunt

 **FriesenPress**

Suite 300 - 990 Fort St
Victoria, BC, Canada, V8V 3K2
www.friesenpress.com

Copyright © 2008 by Rose A. Hunt
First Edition — 2015

ISBN
978-1-4602-6258-0 (Hardcover)
978-1-4602-6259-7 (Paperback)
978-1-4602-6260-3 (eBook)

1. Biography & Autobiography

Distributed to the trade by The Ingram Book Company

For my children

Ramona, Gabriel, and Leonel

They have exemplified every aspect

of the "PDRLs of Life"

CONTENTS

A MOTHER'S ODE

O, mother of noble character
Your eyes bare the witness of great peace
And beauty
You are worth far more than
Diamonds and rubies
Your heart carries more strength
Than the strongest storms
Even your flaws are equivalent
To the stroke of an artist's brush
You gracefully walk slowly with confidence
But if someone where to bring harm to your family
You would strike like a cobra
You work hard for long hours
Sometimes into the darkness of midnight
But your family never has to worry about
Being famished or parched
For they can rely on the Lord
And your noble character alone

Inspired by Proverbs 31
Written by Gabrielle Erwin

MOM 🍎 3MD

A Mother's Story

Gabriel, Sr. and Rose Ann on their wedding day

Foreword

As this world experiences many challenges with parenting, I am delighted to support this great work which is truly a mother's story of triumph over tragedy, and of victory over defeat.

I applaud the life journey of this young mother who was left with three young children to raise after the untimely death of their father. She dedicated herself to them and made many sacrifices to ensure their education, which brought them hope and opportunity. She demonstrated first and foremost that, whatever challenges we face, we can live in harmony with the natural world and bequeath its riches to future generations; furthermore, she exemplified how we can live with each other, bridging the divide of ethnicity, religion, and cultural differences. Thus she equipped her children with skills that allowed them to develop into the professionals they are today.

I am proud to have discovered my sister—the author of this fine book—later in our lives. May she hold her head high and be proud of her great achievement: rearing three brilliant doctors who followed in their father's footsteps, choosing paths that benefit mankind. Like all mothers around the world, the author must be congratulated in the rearing of nation builders who contribute to the well-being of their respective communities.

I wish my beloved sister, Rose, every success with this work, and consider its offering to others as a very necessary and deserving cause.

Paul H. Farquharson, Q. P. M.
High Commissioner of The Bahamas to London and Europe

Preface

The years I spent as a single parent were the most productive times of my life. After the premature death of my husband at the age of thirty-three, I was left with three small children, ages five, six, and seven. I felt there was no way in which I could raise them all alone. But strength came from unexpected places and from surprising events.

Once I remembered that many people had walked down this very road before me and that death is a natural part of life, existing without my soul mate took on a very different light. I buckled in to make life as rewarding for myself and our children as possible, determined to appreciate all the facets of motherhood.

To all you single parents out there who are at their wits' end, endeavoring to make sense of the meaning of parenting, I offer my compassion, words of wisdom, and empathy. I have experienced most of the situations in which you will find yourselves. I offer to you the confidence which comes in reaching goals and the fortitude you will earn by setting the bar as high as you possibly can.

Remember: children need love, discipline, dedication, examples—and above all else, viable role models. There are no better role models for our children than parents who are dedicated to making the many sacrifices needed in order to create a positive environment for them; parents who are willing to do whatever it takes to make their world a better place in which to thrive.

Some things worked with my children; others did not. And I found that my own wisdom increased as I listened to what my children had to say, letting them be my teachers on occasion.

My greatest desire in writing this first book in the series of MOM3MD is to reach out to parents raising children—whether with a partner or alone—as well as to the children, grandparents, teachers, and clergymen with whom they come in contact. In essence, this book is for anyone who wants to positively influence the lives of the young people entrusted to their care.

May you find hope, courage, understanding, faith, joy, and love as you read the saga which unfolds within these pages.

Rose A. Hunt

Photograph by Bronson Photography, Glendale CA

CHAPTER 1

The Hand That Rocked My Cradle

The scent of Arpège by Lanvin always takes me back to that December day in 1955. I was but six years old, yet decades later this fragrance still invokes her memory.

She was the vision of loveliness in her pale vanilla dress coat over a black velvet suit, its collar wrapped in pure white satin. When my eyes followed the hem of her coat, I could see the silk stockings which covered her long legs down to her black patent-leather pumps. Her posture this day, as always, was erect; her chin was uplifted, and her eyes kind but determined. And her own fragrance, mingled with the Lanvin, was that of roses, oranges, candy, cake, and everything delightful to a child. These are the smells of Mother, of home. She walked at her always-hurried pace to catch the Number 29 train to Fort Pierce, Florida, after we departed the plane from Nassau, Bahamas. My six-year-old stride no match for her own, I never ceased having to ask my mother to please slow down.

No one ever guessed that Mother sewed all her own clothes, as well as mine. I wore a brand-new red flannel suit, the softest fabric I had ever touched. My short jacket was accented with three medium-sized, white mushroom buttons. The pure white poplin blouse had a Peter Pan collar that covered a round, collarless jacket. My pigtails hung long on my shoulders, and were emphasized by a full-cut bang across my forehead. Right in the middle of my face was a two-inch scar, a continual reminder of a serious fall I had taken at the age of three.

The pigtails spilled out from beneath a white Tami sham which protected my head from the cold, crisp air. My feet, moving frantically to keep up with Mother, were encased in snow-white nylon socks and black patent-leather shoes. We could have been on one of Norman Rockwell's *Saturday Evening Post* covers, she in her white coat and I in my red, rushing to catch our train.

Mackey Airlines had not been on time with the flight from Nassau, Bahamas to Miami, Florida, and so Mother hurried for good reason: train number 29 was leaving the station just as we approached. This made Mother all the more frantic as she knew there would not be another train for some hours. She quickened her already-fast stride to a near sprint, and my feet occasionally missed the ground as they matched Mother's haste.

"All aboard," we heard the conductor bellow as the train started to slowly move along the rails. Mother's white coat and my red coat were but a blur now, and Mother had all but given up when the train came to an abrupt halt. The conductor beckoned for us to hurry, and we reached the steps and boarded the train. Mother was appreciative of the conductor, and I couldn't help but exclaim, "I don't believe we made the train stop for us!" Surely we were important people!

CHAPTER 2

A Whole New World

I hesitantly exited the taxicab and stood outside the door of a place that immediately struck me as heavenly. A man approached, arms outstretched, to greet us. He was about the same height as Mother and wore a gray shirt and pants. The shirt had something red on the pocket, and he smelled of something I could not recognize.

I hid inside Mother's coat. The man scared me. Who was he, and what did he want from us? But he swept my trembling body up in his arms and walked toward this heavenly abode—a white house with green trim, a home right out of a storybook.

The heady scent of roses seemed to surround us, and the grass was greener than any I had known back home. A hedge outlined the whole house where the grass ended. Just inside the hedge, at the left-hand corner of the house, a bed of multicolored flowers burst from the ground. Yes, this had to be heaven. My fear of the man who carried me quickly turned to awe, for surely he was my guardian angel.

He carried me up the front steps into an enclosed porch—something I had never seen before—and there the man put me down. Mother took my hand and led me from the porch into the living room. It smelled like the outdoors, fresh and clean. The floor was made of the shiniest, smoothest boards ever! A rug lay in front of a very long chair. Another big, short chair was next to a table in one corner. Yet another big chair was in the other corner, next to a table and lamp of the same kind.

I was led to a room, and I gasped at its prettiness. The pale-green walls were covered with tiny sparkles. A west-facing and a southern-exposed window were both curtained in white, sheer fabric. In the middle of the room stood a bed. A big bed. A bedside table held a lamp, its lampshade bordered in tiny yellow, blue, and pink flowers.

No one spoke as I looked around the room. I spied a dresser with a mirror in one corner. And to the right of the dresser stood a chest of drawers. Later, I learned the names of all these astonishing pieces of furniture, things I had never seen before. I kept walking around the room, close to Mother.

Taking a shy peek at the man, I noticed something on the bed. It was the most beautiful doll—actually, the *only* doll—I had ever seen up close! I approached the doll and reached out to grab it, but stopped. I guessed it must belong to a little girl who lived here, and I wondered where that little girl might be.

Mother picked up the doll and bent down in front of me, as did the man in the gray clothes.

"This is for you," they said. "She belongs to you."

I cried, but they were not tears of joy. I was afraid to take the doll. No one had ever given me a present.

The man in the gray clothes tried to comfort me, but I only cried more. Soon Mother and the man backed away, not knowing what else to do. The man said he had to go back to work, and had turned to go when Mother stopped him.

"This is your daddy," she said to me. "And I am your mommy now. You are our little girl."

My tears stopped abruptly. The man and woman took me in their arms. I had never had a daddy before.

Mother said, "Rose Ann, you can call him Daddy, okay?"

I could not believe my ears. This woman who had taken care of me in the Bahamas, the one to whom I had become so attached in my six years of visits with her, was not just "Mother" but *my own* special mommy now. And the man in the gray clothes was my daddy.

My biological mother had decided long before details were completed to let her first cousin—the woman I now called Mother—raise me as her own. The Bahamas at that time was foreign territory, so there were numerous steps to be taken before I could be allowed to live in the United States. Each time Mother visited me, she had to return to her home in Fort Pierce alone. It had been sheer torture for us both. But the wait was over. I was home at last.

That night I fell right to sleep.

CHAPTER 3

Dawn of a New Day

In the morning, I awoke to the aroma of food cooking. I wondered if it was all a dream, but I discovered it was not as I got out of bed and followed my nose to the kitchen, where Daddy prepared a breakfast of grits and scrambled eggs, chipped beef in a creamy sauce, and biscuits.

"Good morning, Rose Ann. You should wash up and brush your teeth before breakfast," he said.

When I walked back to my room, Mother was already there, setting out my clothes for the day. There was a lot to do in preparation for school. Mother gave me a big hug and helped me get cleaned up and dressed for breakfast.

Never before had I sat down to a breakfast that was anything but cornflakes and water mixed with canned milk. And I had never tasted eggs, grits, or homemade biscuits. In fact, I had not been trained in any table etiquette, for I had always sat on the floor to eat. I had no idea what to do with the fork and knife; I always ate everything with a spoon. Mother had her work cut out for her.

Daddy was off to work at Sunrise Lumber Company where he was employed as a truck driver. I was not happy to see him go, even though he had not said much to me that morning. But I felt important around him.

Early that afternoon, Mother took me to visit Margaret and Ossie Paige. They were family friends and would be a great help to me. Mrs. Paige had spent many days making telephone calls to the school board of St. Lucie County in her quest to help me get into school.

It was, after all, the end of the first semester. School was out for the Christmas holiday. And as Mrs. Paige learned from that first visit, I had no idea what school was, having never been in a classroom. Therefore, I would not know how to handle being confined to a desk for most of a school day. I did not yet know my alphabet, and I was not acquainted with numbers. These adults, my new family and friends and teachers, had an interesting challenge ahead of them.

When Daddy came home from work, he was informed of the necessary steps which had to be taken before I could go to first grade. I was much too old for kindergarten, and he never considered putting me anywhere but in the right classroom for my age.

The *ABC Primer* and *Alice and Jerry* books became my constant friends for the next two weeks. Learning the alphabet was the greatest challenge. Daddy was so very patient with me. It seemed I would never get the difference between the letters E and P. Mommy and Daddy labored tirelessly for the next two weeks in preparation for the test necessary for me to enter first grade.

CHAPTER 4

First Lessons

Ms. Ford, the first grade teacher at Lincoln Park Academy, was very impressed when I passed with flying colors. Not only did I complete the test, but I went on to finish the grade with the rest of the class.

Daddy was so proud of me that he took us to the Dairy Queen for ice cream. Our regular Sunday afternoon rides in our new car always ended in a visit to the local ice cream parlor.

I lived for these times with my parents. Daddy would drive around to visit friends and relatives. (I think it was just to show off the car.) I loved having the back seat all to myself. I could curl up when I was sleepy, or I would stretch out; still there would be enough room for my dolls. I always took them with me.

Upon a recent visit to my hometown, I was sad to learn that the Dairy Queen in the location across the street from what was St. Anastasia School had disappeared. I felt it should have been made a historic monument. I was happy to learn that one had opened not far from my parents, though it was not the same. I had so many wonderful memories of the place, and it was at Dairy Queen that I was first introduced to the reality of racism in the United States of America.

After one of our rides, Daddy went to the window to get our ice cream. As was my custom, I exited the car and turned to the water fountain to get a drink. I had never paid attention to the words written above the two fountains until then: "White Water" to the left and "Colored Water" above the fountain on the right. Well, I did not want colored water. I'd never had colored water before and was not willing to try it right now when I was so thirsty.

When I returned to the car with my ice cream cone in hand, I asked Daddy what the signs meant. He explained to me that *colored* meant people like us. People like the governor and his wife and my friends who lived on the beach were called *white*. They didn't look white to me, but who was I to question what my daddy said? Anyway, all was right with my world. The grownups could handle all the colored and white stuff.

I informed him that I had a drink from the "white water" fountain. He replied, "The water is no different. You can always drink from whichever fountain you care to as long as your mother or I am with you." That was that. I admit I never did try the colored water. I had my suspicions.

I still know where all the Dairy Queens are located, no matter where I have lived. It is the place I go to for comfort food.

The county library was my next most favorite place to visit. My mother took me there to get books. When I reached my ninth birthday, I was able to sign my name on my own library card. It was one of the most memorable days of my life up to that point. Every Thursday I would walk to the library after school to return books and check out new ones. I was soon reading as many as five books a week.

I had no idea that none of the other students in my class ever visited the library. It had never entered my mind that they were under the impression that the "colored" children were not allowed. The librarian was always very nice and helpful to me. She allowed me to choose the books I enjoyed reading without any problem. Once, when my daddy came to the library to get me after work, we sat and read for a while before we went home. If there was a problem, I never knew about it.

CHAPTER 5

Lessons in Obedience

My first experience with the consequences of disobedience came one day after school at the end of the week. The neighbor girl, Margaret, had always escorted me home. She was in the second grade. I had become fascinated with the playground equipment and never could get enough play time when my class went to recess.

Margaret and I played a bit after school on the swings and merry-go-round. But what I really wanted to do was climb the steps to the huge slide and experience the wind in my face as I slid down. I was unable to influence Margaret to stay any longer, and she took off down the path for home.

Time was not important to me that day. It did not occur to me that I did not know my way home as I watched Margaret disappear around the bend in the path leading away from the school. It also did not matter that I was the only child on the playground, nor that it was beginning to get dark. I had no thoughts of home until I was at the top of the slide for the last time and saw a familiar figure in the distance.

The figure was coming very fast in my direction—it was Mother. When she approached the school playground, I got the most disturbing feeling in the pit of my stomach. My backside began to itch when I ascertained what was in her hand.

Waving a belt above her head, she came to me with more anguish than anger. Then there was sheer relief on her face as she stood in front of me. I was never more happy and scared at the same time. The events of that afternoon stood at the forefront of my memory for a long time. Especially reminiscent is the hurt inflicted on my backside as I ran ahead of my mother on our way home. I was fast, but she had longer legs.

The end of the belt met with my rear end several times before we got home. As a matter of fact, I believe the only thing that saved me from another conversation with the belt was that my daddy was too relieved that I was safe to spank me.

There were so many more lessons just like this one that taught me the meaning of strict obedience. I would learn them all! The lessons I learned from my parents would make an indelible impression on the way I would train my own children. I am eternally grateful for those difficult lessons.

I recall yet another incident when it was necessary to be reminded of how much easier it is to obey than compromise. It was Easter Sunday, and my mother had given permission for me to attend services at Mount Olive Missionary Baptist Church with one of our neighbors. She had made a very special dress for me. It was aqua blue embroidered taffeta. The empire waistline was accented with a long, pink velvet ribbon, tied into a huge bow right in the front. The puffed sleeves were banded with piping. The accessories included white patent-leather shoes, pink socks, and a brand-new pair of white gloves. I carried a white, bucket-shaped, draw-string purse adorned with pink flowers. Mother had made certain I was eye candy that day. She had put my hair up in French curls for the occasion.

As Beulah (my teenage neighbor) and I left to walk the long distance to the church, Mother's final words of wisdom were, "Make sure you two go straight to church and come straight back home."

Well, on the way to church, we passed a very loaded mulberry tree. There were so many juicy, black mulberries that we just had to have at least one or two. There could be no harm in that, could there? I was all of eight years old at the time. How was I to know that I should take my gloves off before picking the berries? In my excitement, I did not think.

By the time we noticed we would be late for church if we stayed any longer, it was already too late. Beulah took one look at me and shook her finger as she said, "You are going to get a whuppin' when you get home." I became heartsick with worry. Not only did I disobey, but I was now totally filthy and had missed church.

Needless to say, my dress was ruined. Mulberry stains do not come out—*that* I learned on Easter Sunday, 1957. Even though my belly was full with the sweet, juicy berries, my heart was filled with dread. Daddy and Mother were not pleased and made it known by the punishment I received . . . a lesson I have never forgotten.

I learned the best lesson of all in obedience on a particularly memorable day as I arrived home from school. I noticed that the cherry hedge bordering the front yard was full of ripe cherries. Mother would allow me to pick them only after the cherries were deep red in color. This meant they were perfect for eating.

But even though the cherries were not quite dark enough, they were so very tempting, and my mouth began to water in anticipation of the succulent juices bursting with flavor. So as I walked along the hedge, I pulled cherries, eating as fast as I pulled.

Not only was I not to pick them until they were ready, but I was also supposed to rinse them before eating. The hedge was sometimes sprayed with insecticide. If Mother ever found out, she would not be happy. But little did I know that Mother had noticed me from a bedroom window; she watched with disappointment as I scarfed down the deliciously tart cherries.

I hurriedly went around to the back of the house, where I washed my hands under the water spigot. I was shocked when Mother greeted me at the back door. She asked about my day at school, as she often did, once I was inside the house. I walked into my bedroom and she followed me, taking a seat on my bed. Her next question caught me quite off-guard as I stepped out of my green plaid skirt.

"Rose Ann, did I not ask you not to eat those cherries before they get ripe?"

"What cherries?" I asked innocently, without looking at her. "I just came home from school." I stalled for time. I needed to figure out what to say. Did she know I had eaten the cherries?

The patient, quiet way in which she questioned me did not give me the answer. My mother never raised her voice. She was not familiar with the screaming tactics of other parents I had heard, so I was at a loss as to reading her. It took me a few years to become familiar with her parenting techniques, but I learned from her lessons that I would carry out with my own children.

I tried, without success, to talk my way out of a severe punishment. I had to listen to a lecture about deception and theft. Mother made me feel as if I had committed the unpardonable sin, but in the most quiet, loving tone imaginable. The physical punishment would be executed once Daddy got home from work and before dinner, so I would have a most uncomfortable dinner in store for me.

I learned that it is always best to tell the truth, no matter the consequences. I learned that deception could lead to many unsavory consequences. Mother said that a liar would eventually steal, and that a thief would eventually become a murderer. Did I want to become any one of these? No, I did not.

I had yet another opportunity to learn a lesson in obedience. When I was nine years old, my mother taught me to wash and iron my own clothing. We had a washing machine, but I learned to wash by hand using a scrub board. Each Sunday morning, I would rise early to begin my laundering. I would fill three big galvanized tubs with water—one for washing, two for rinsing. Another smaller tub was used for starching. After my clothes were hung on the line to dry, I would get the ironing board set up in order to iron. By nightfall, all laundering would be completely done, with clothes ironed and hung in my closet.

Of course, there were certain dresses that were more difficult to iron than others. One particular dress had an underskirt which had a ruffled hemline. This ruffle was very difficult to handle, especially when starched. My mother did not believe in "cat faces," which were folds made in the fabric when the iron was pushed along without first straightening the cloth. I was tired and had left this dress for last. I deliberately passed the iron very lightly over the ruffle without taking care not to press any wrinkles.

The next morning, Mother decided I should wear this same dress to school. I knew I was in trouble when she made this special request. As I was leaving for school, she stopped to ask if I had pressed the underskirt of the dress. It looked rough-dried to her. I replied that I had. She was not happy with the result.

She asked that I take it off and properly press the dress. My feelings showed on my face as I reminded her I would be late for school. "Well, in that case, you will wear it inside out so that everyone will see how carelessly you feel about your clothing. And you better not turn it over when you get to school, because I will know!"

After that episode, I can truthfully say I have become an expert at pressing clothes, and many have complimented me on this talent. I have even been told I should open a laundry. Imagine that! Mother always told me that if I did anything at all, that I was to do it right or not at all. This I endeavored to remember.

CHAPTER 6

Learning More About Life

In addition to caring for garments, I also learned to care for animals. We had chickens, turkeys, and hound dogs. It became one of my chores to feed the chickens, collect the hens' eggs, and provide them with fresh water every day. Daddy taught me to clean out the drinking buckets every day and showed me how to get the hens to come up from the eggs once they were laid.

There were different kinds of chickens in the pen with multiple dispositions. I was at odds with one special hen, and she just had to be the one who laid the most eggs. Whenever I tried to gather her eggs, she would peck me mercilessly. I often fought back by chasing her around the pen and grabbing at her tail. I hated that hen! I was glad when she suddenly disappeared from the yard. I had a suspicious feeling she wound up on our dinner plates.

And then there were the turkeys. I had never seen a turkey before I came to my new life. I thought these big birds were the most ridiculous things I could have imagined. They were so ugly, I thought. And they smelled worse than the chickens. They were almost as tall as I, and I did not like it! The turkeys would grab at the food before I had a chance to get it completely out of the feeding bucket I carried. Thank God I didn't have to collect eggs from them! No way would I want that chore.

The chickens were amusing to watch. Sometimes I would spend a little more time in the yard than necessary after the egg harvesting and feeding was done. I especially enjoyed watching the chicks hatch from the eggs that were left in the nest. This happened during the times my daddy would collect eggs. He knew which ones to leave in the nest.

My daddy was the best daddy in the whole world as far as I was concerned. He was so proud of me and so happy that he now had his very own little girl. I loved him with all my heart. He made me feel like I was the most important child in the universe.

In order to expose me to the world around me, my father would take me on fishing expeditions. I learned to bait a hook, cast a line, and bring in my fish. And after many a wounded finger, I became proficient at removing the hook from my own catch. It became a family ritual for us to go fishing with the Paiges: my cousin, Kielier, her Aunt Hussein, and our friend, Barbara Ann. We would set out very early in the mornings in order to find a great fishing spot where we could also have a picnic.

Of course, we had everything needed for cleaning, frying, and eating our catch of the day. Daddy was always sure to have plenty of fresh, clean water on hand for us. I especially enjoyed the hush puppies made according to his recipes. He could batch up a slew of those things that would make you cry, they were just that good! Mother would bake cookies and pound cakes to entice us to fish more so we would have enough fish to take home with us.

It was important to her for me to keep up with my class, so she brought the primary reading books along. When I was not fishing with my daddy, she would spread out a blanket and read to me under the Australian pines. She especially read poems written by Poe, Frost, Whitman, and Shelley. It was not until I was much older that I would recite from memory lines from most of the poetry or sometimes the entire works. James Weldon Johnson's "Creation" comes readily to mind. It was one of my favorites.

It was no small wonder that I began to enjoy the time sitting at my mother's knee as she read story after story to me. After time spent in this way, I was able to read for myself, and became an avid reader. I finished Tolstoy's *War and Peace* in record time during my freshman year in high school, as well as *Gone with the Wind* that same year. I still have trouble passing up an opportunity to curl up with a good book.

Daddy became adept at taking care of me in my mother's absence. He could comb and brush my hair, get me dressed for school, and take me shopping for new shoes. He never had to buy anything else since my mother was an excellent seamstress who made all of my clothing. She was so good with a needle and thread that she was asked to work on the governor's wife's inaugural ball gown!

I had an idyllic childhood. Although I was in a one-child household, there were always children around the house, as often I would collect the neighborhood children to play in my yard. It was the biggest yard around—big enough to support a game of baseball, kickball, or hide-and-seek without going into the street.

In addition, our yard was the only yard that contained a variety of fruits all year round. There were three different types of mangoes, and there was a hedge of cherries, a mulberry tree, loquats, and guavas. My mother always had a supply of jelly, which she hand-made, from each of these fruit trees. All the neighborhood children knew where to find good eating. I never lacked company or attention.

The southeastern corner of our house was a spot designed by Daddy just for roses. He was a natural at growing things, so the roses flourished, along with the many ixora, phlox, zinnias, and countless other flowering bushes I could not name. Every evening, upon his return from working all day, Daddy would stay in the yard taking care of his flowers and lawn. We had the most beautiful yard in the neighborhood, according to our neighbors. No matter the time of year, something was always in bloom at the Bakers' home.

Keeping the plants watered soon became one of the chores I enjoyed most. I also quickly learned how to keep the surrounding shrubbery free from weeds. My mother was a very good teacher when it came to showing me how to pull the weeds from their roots, rather than the tops. I looked forward to taking care of this job. I especially wondered at the growth of flowers from seeds. The whole process amazed me.

Soon I was planting my own garden in a spot Mother prepared for me on the north side of the house. Sometimes I was successful, and sometimes not. But it wasn't long before I could tell when my seedlings needed water or when weeds were crowding the roots underground. All of this was an exciting project for me. I could grow anything. I finally had a green thumb, which I have never lost; I can still grow anything.

CHAPTER 7

Grandma Alice

During the summertime, my mother and I would visit my grandmother and aunt in Nassau, Bahamas. My grandmother, Alice, owned a restaurant on Shirley Street. We always stayed at her house, which was in the same yard as the restaurant.

I remember getting up early in the mornings to "help" her get the restaurant going for the day. She would cook pigeon peas and rice, fried chicken, plantains, and desserts of all kinds. I especially liked to watch her make the tarts, which were her specialty. My favorite was the pineapple.

She even made her own brand of toffee candy for sale. It was so much fun to watch her bake. My mother inherited her culinary skills. I had my share of homemade cookies and cake to put in my lunch for school, most of which was eaten by my classmates as I did not have a significant sweet tooth during my childhood.

When Grandmother Alice baked, she always let me clean the baking dishes. There was always a little something left in them for me, especially the candy dishes! I also learned to keep the restaurant neat and clean after customers. I enjoyed being around my grandmother, and I was so sad when she died shortly after my eleventh birthday.

Mother made sure I was kept busy during the time spent in the Bahamas. She sent me to learn crocheting with a lady who lived not far from Grandmother Alice. I was able to walk there by myself every morning. I did not take well to the process, and my teacher did not appreciate this.

"The lil' gal can't lu'n," she told Mother in her Bahamian vernacular. This phrase became a private joke between Mother and me as I got older. It was a glorious day when I finally did learn to crochet. I was so very proud of myself; I did *lu'n* after all.

Grandma Alice was responsible for a strange habit I carry to this day: I will not drink water from any beverage glass. Grandma Alice wore dentures; in order to keep them clean, she would soak them overnight in a glass much like those she used in the restaurant. I only know this because I accidentally came upon the dentures soaking in the glass of water on the table by Grandma Alice's bedroom door as I arose much earlier than usual one morning. I believe the glass was placed there in haste as she had prepared for bed the previous night. She took special pains to prevent me from ever seeing her without her teeth.

The very next day, after seeing those dentures in the glass, I could not drink anything. Sometimes still, as an adult, I find it difficult to drink from similar glasses. Who says what you learn in childhood is sometimes lost? I don't think so!

Grandmother Alice was a strict disciplinarian, and I did not escape her scrutiny. She was a firm believer in unquestionable obedience and felt that children were to be seen and not heard unless they were spoken to or had asked permission to speak.

On occasions, during my summer trips, I stayed with my Aunt Rose and Daddy George. Daddy George, as he was affectionately called by the family, was married to my mother's older sister, Rosalie. They lived in a big house on St. James Road. This was not too far from my grandmother's house.

There was a huge guinep tree in Aunt Rose's front yard, which was always laden with fruit during the summer. I had a passion for fruit of any kind. This yard, like my yard back in Fort Pierce, was a fruit temptation haven for children. It was home to sapodilla, sugar apple, and sour sop fruit trees, and the temptation to eat as much as I could of each fruit, each day, would prove to become my undoing.

The guinep fruit was a favorite among Bahamian children. The children would sell bunches to tourists along the island streets. The only drawback was that if clothing was stained by the juice, it would become permanently imbedded into the fabric, never to disappear again.

One night, as I prepared for bed, my stomach was in such turmoil that I thought I would surely die before daybreak. I lay down, thinking it would soon subside. It did not. Mother heard me whining and writhing in bed and came to investigate. I was burning up with fever. She hurriedly attended to bringing the fever down.

By and by, I attempted to relieve my colon, but with no success. I was severely constipated. For such a little girl, this was extremely painful. My stomach was protruding from my body; I was in the worst pain! What to do?

It was time to bring out the "worm refuse." This was the Bahamian prescription for children who were susceptible to parasitic worms. Parents often relayed to their children that these parasites came from eating too much candy, thus serving a two-fold purpose.

In any event, my immediate problem was getting to go to the bathroom without pain. Mother gave me some of the dreaded medicine, and we waited. I was finally able to get some sleep, but by morning, the pain had returned. It was time for the next course of action.

When I saw the "spirits of turpentine" bottle on the table beside my bed, I immediately knew what was coming next. By the time Mother walked

into the room with the teaspoon and sugar jar in her hands, I was resigned
to my fate.

"Good morning, Rose Ann. How is my little girl feeling this morning?"
She waited for my answer while checking my forehead to gauge my tem-
perature. I attempted to make my face show what my body was not feeling.
"Okay," was my quiet answer.

"Your fever is gone. Did you have a bowel movement when you went
to the toilet this morning?" she questioned. I did not answer right away, so
she reached under the cover and felt my tummy. This was not a good sign.
My abdomen was still very swollen, even though I was not in pain.

As Mother encouraged me to get up and use the toilet, I was filled with
dismay. She had that knowing look in her eyes which told me the medicine
was forthcoming, whether I was successful in having a bowel movement or
not. The trip to the toilet was unsuccessful, to say the least.

I would have sat there all day, if only I could avoid the "medicine." And
to add insult to injury, Mother was soon standing at the door to the bathroom to make sure I did not try to slip one by her.

It was not until she brought the white bed bucket to my bedside that I
knew I was in for the whole nine yards of treatment: spirits of turpentine,
followed by an enema! Mother was determined to clean out whatever was
making me sick.

When she opened the sugar jar and pulled out a teaspoonful of sugar, I knew
instantly it had begun. She even asked me to hand her the turpentine bottle, as
if the anxiety was not excruciating enough. Too late now! The time had come!

I obediently swallowed the teaspoonful of sugar, laced with one drop of
turpentine. It was the vilest and sweetest thing I had ever experienced. If
any parasite could survive this, I would be surprised! I lay back down on
my bed and waited.

It was not long before I had to race to sit on the bucket as I felt my stomach begin to churn. Suddenly, my bowels gave way, and a long sigh of emotional as well as physical release swept over me. This sudden release had made me very weak, so I fell back onto my bed as mother surveyed the damage. I knew instantly by the way she slowly backed away from the scene that whatever was in the bucket was not good.

It was my Aunt Rose who braved the unknown and took a look. "I told you that this child was full of worms!" she triumphantly proclaimed. Mother was already out of the room and in another part of the house. I was left alone to bear the burden of listening to my aunt's sermon regarding disobedience, healthy eating, and cleanliness. After all, who was left to take care of me and the mess I had created? She and I.

It was much later on, as I grew into the teenage years, before I attempted to try another guinep. I was also very cautious in my choice of desserts long into adulthood. I endeavored to keep the parasites away and have had no repeats of that morning. I consider myself truly blessed!

Mother would sometimes come for the week when it was time to go back home. I had such wonderful summers, but I was always ready to return home to the United States in preparation for school in the fall.

One summer, while in Nassau, I spent a couple of weeks with my biological mother and two sisters. I enjoyed being with them, though my older sister and I fought a lot. She claimed I was too bossy; I told her she was too whiny. I later understood that what I meant was that she was too passive; she did not like confrontation.

Rocking the boat was not her forte—but *I* did not mind rocking the boat if it meant I could get across the river much faster. My younger sister at the time was much too young to care or understand. Therefore we got along very well then and still do.

I never knew my biological father since he died when I was a baby and was not married to my mother. The only things I heard about him came from other family members. He was employed as a teacher. I was told I "favored" (resembled) him a lot. He died as the result of a medical error during a tonsillectomy. He also had a son, a few months older than I. My brother and I eventually found each other as adults, and I am happy we did. He has turned out to be everything a sister could want in a brother.

CHAPTER 8

Lessons on Death and Dying

Two years after my adoptive father passed away, my biological mother died at a very young age after becoming very ill with an incurable disease. I was sad, but I did not want to go to her funeral. I begged my adopted mother not to make me go, and thankfully, she did not force me to attend. Furthermore, Mother did not go because I did not want her to leave me. Even though Eva was her first cousin biologically, my mother stayed home with me. I have appreciated her decision.

There were many relatives, as well as others, who questioned why I was not at the funeral. I believe they blamed Mother as being the reason. But she did not let them bother her. She did what she thought was best for her little girl; in this case, she chose not to traumatize me any more than necessary. I loved my mother!

I came home one day when I was nine years old to find my mother gone. She was always at home when I returned from school each day, so I became alarmed at her absence. Our only neighbor to the north of our house sent her son down to bring me to their house. I was informed that my father had taken sick and was at the hospital. Upon her return later that evening, Mother broke the news of my daddy's illness.

During visiting hours, I was allowed to see him in the hospital. I missed him so at home. I did not expect events in my life to change so abruptly. He was always glad to see me, and I wondered why it was taking so long for him to come home. When he was finally home, it was for only a short time; he was soon whisked off to Jackson Memorial Hospital in Miami, 120 miles away from where we lived. Now I would not be able to see him whenever I wanted to.

It became increasingly more difficult for me to understand this illness that kept my daddy away from my mother and me. I was very sad. My teacher, Mrs. Todd, did all she could to cheer me up, but to no avail. My classmates were so good to me. It was as if they really understood what I was going through.

On February 14, 1959—Valentine's Day—I had one last conversation with the very first man in my life to make me a significant part of his world. He told me he was going away and that he was not coming home. At first, I did not realize he was saying good-bye to me for the very last time, so I did not feel sad about his remarks. I convinced myself that he was just going to another hospital and would come back home again soon.

It was my mother who had to console me when she made me understand the true meaning of his words. It was the worst day of my short life, thus far. The pain I felt drove deep down inside my heart where nothing else could reach.

After the funeral, I kept my tears to myself; I did not want to cause my mother any more unhappiness or concern than she was already enduring. I became good at masking my feelings. I loved my mother deeply, and I missed my daddy terribly.

Whatever would we do without him? Who would take me fishing? Who would teach me not to be afraid of wild animals? Who would take me shopping for shoes? Who would take me hunting in the woods? Who would make me laugh at his jokes? Who else would be so very proud to take me visiting with him, happy to have his little girl by his side? I was completely devastated.

In addition to my activities with the neighborhood children, I began bringing home stray dogs, cats, or whatever I found. In some ways, I redirected love for my father into compassion toward animals in need of care. This helped a lot with my grief.

I suppose, in part, the experience I gathered from taking care of the kids who were much younger than I prepared me for the job of parenting, and helped to relieve the pain caused by losing my father. I learned to bathe, dress, and braid my neighbor's twin girls' hair when I was just ten years old. I could change a diaper better than most adults.

In the short time I had my daddy, he taught me about life, people, plants, animals, and good and evil. A kid could not ask for more. And at times over the years, whenever I have had a most difficult decision to make, I withdraw moments from my memory vault and think of him. I often ask myself the question, "What would Daddy tell me to do?"

On Saturday mornings, I would make my rounds in order to have children to take to church with me. Otherwise, I was the only child in the church. And then on Saturday afternoons, after dinner, I would start all over again for the evening service. I found immense pleasure in doing for others. I soon began remembering the good times, though cut short, that I got to spend with my daddy.

Whenever I am at home in Fort Pierce, I can still find quiet and solitude at his gravesite. The quiet time away from everything and everybody bring peace and comfort—and many times, it brings good answers, too.

CHAPTER 9

Beginning Again

Religion played a major role in my upbringing. I went to church with Mother every Saturday morning; she was Seventh-day Adventist, while Daddy was Baptist. Before we got our first car, Mother and I would walk the twelve blocks to Avenue "E" and Macedonia. She was Sabbath School secretary, and we were always there before 9:00 a.m. Song service began promptly at 9:15.

The very first time I went to this church, there were eight adult members. There was not a single other child; I was the only one. They were happy to have a new member, and I could tell they were happy that my mother now had her very own little girl. She showed pride in the way she meticulously dressed me; I was always dressed in the finest Irish linen, cotton gingham, dotted Swiss, and 100-percent cashmere sweater outfits.

Nothing was ordinary about my wardrobe! I always wore a wristwatch, even before I could tell time. My watch was given to me by my Aunt Rose and her husband, on my eighth birthday. He had bought it in Switzerland on one of his band tours. Even though I had everything a child could possibly want, I was not a "spoiled brat." I was just loved beyond measure, and my parents took every opportunity to let me know it.

Even when I was disciplined severely for misdeeds, I knew I was loved by the tears that welled up in my daddy's eyes. I felt his reluctance to reprimand me, which made me want to try harder to be good. I often thought, *If there really is a heaven, then I know Daddy will be there.*

Church for me was lonely until I canvassed my neighborhood and surrounding areas, including my classmates, to attend church with us. Soon there were so many children we could out-sing all the adults. Eventually, the parents of some of the children began attending, soon becoming members.

But now the hard task of providing fell to my mother alone. She knew it would be better with a male influence around to help her raise me, so she remarried four years after my daddy died. After having my mother all to myself, I was not too happy to share her with someone else. It might have been much more difficult had I not known the man she would consider for marriage. She even asked my opinion on the matter, and I voiced my thoughts. I came home from school one day, and they were married.

My stepfather was a wonderful provider; however, he was not experienced at parenting. He tested my boundaries; I tested his—and we still do to this day. The more things change, the more they stay the same. I give him respect and honor for giving my mother a chance at happiness, which would have eluded her otherwise. Who else would have put up with the feelings of a thirteen-year-old girl who blamed the world for taking her father away? I was too afraid to blame God.

As far as I was concerned, my stepfather tried much too hard (and way too fast) to replace my daddy. It was overwhelming for me to handle, and I became frustrated and ambivalent toward him.

Additionally, his ex-girlfriend had just delivered a baby boy, leading me to wonder if this man could be trusted. If he could leave a pregnant woman stranded with his baby, could he not also leave us if he chose to later on down the line? In light of this, I would not let myself trust him. But he insisted the child did not belong to him, even though he signed the birth certificate, giving the boy his last name.

I was quite confused with this chain of events, and I questioned my mother about her feelings regarding the baby. She made an attempt to dissuade my suspicions about her new husband, but even so, I never fully trusted him.

It was a power struggle all the way, but we soon learned to coexist in a peaceful manner. I even took it upon myself to teach him to read and write properly. My mother taught him to drive. I introduced him to the game of checkers. My daddy had taught me well.

While I tried to make sense of the world which I felt took my father away, I became more introverted and skeptical of people around me, especially adults. No one took the time to question me about my feelings, so I coped alone, and became quiet and withdrawn at home.

My mother's marriage and the baby boy were often the topic of conversation around town. I was ashamed whenever it came up. I felt I could no longer talk about the situation with my mother, so I continued to carry the burden of unanswered questions.

I hid my insecurities from my mother; she was busy trying to provide for me as best she could, and I had everything a young woman could possibly imagine, physically. My stepfather was in his own world as local elder of the church, and I am not sure he would have recognized the problem anyway. He paid little attention to anyone or anything but the church and his "church people." He lived to impress them.

Junior high school proved to be a new world for me, and I attempted to fit in with my classmates. I had made some close friends throughout the elementary years, which carried over to junior high, but it was still a challenge. I only saw my friends at school or whenever I visited occasionally.

Our play days were over, and it was time to make a decisive change. With all of this on my mind, I became comfortable at being alone.

The first boy to pay special attention to me was Bruce. It happened when we were in fifth grade. He and I were chosen to represent our class for some event. Afterward, he told me how pretty he thought I was in my new dress. He quickly brushed my cheek with his lips. It was my very first kiss.

Bruce was a handsome and mannerly boy. He was smart, too. I took extra effort not to wash the spot on my left cheek where his lips had hurriedly brushed my skin. *Wow, he really likes me!* I remember thinking.

That same year, I was also chosen to be an attendant to Miss Frances K. Sweet Elementary. That short encounter with Bruce went a long way in boosting my self-confidence. It helped me stand my ground in junior high, even though I was still a bit introverted.

CHAPTER 10

Developing Confidence

The last year of elementary school put the final touches on my self-assuredness. I was chosen to represent the school as May Day queen, and along with Wilbur, the May Day king, it was our job to "reign" over the festivities held in honor of May Day (May 1). I wore a very special dress of white organdy, having three tiers, surrounded by the best lace my mother could find. She spared no expense with this one. I held a scepter in my hand as I sat with my king under a shaded "throne" high above the ground. Wilbur and I made the newspaper that year.

As my confidence grew, the upperclassmen boys began noticing me in a way that made me very uncertain of my new-found confidence. I was not allowed to date, so the attention became more and more disconcerting. I attempted to play the games I noticed the other girls used with the boys but was uncomfortable with the feedback I received. It was against my nature to play shy and helpless now that I had acquired such self-confidence.

I was my mother's only child, her only chance at parenting; I was not about to mess that up. I was careful not to encourage the boys' attention, but it was not an easy task. They seemed to want to talk to me no matter how I ignored them. The more I ignored them, the more attention I received. Something had to be done! So I finally created a strategy: I would find one boy who I knew would not be interested in me, and I'd talk to him. Surely that would keep the others away.

Before I had opportunity to make a decision as to whom I would choose, an upperclassman began paying a lot of attention to me. I learned he was going steady with a girl in the sophomore class, so I felt he just wanted to play games with me. I decided that if I pretended to like him, the other unwanted attention might go away.

He began showing up throughout the day in places where he knew I would be on campus; I enjoyed talking with him once I got to know him. I was not concerned that his steady girlfriend would be upset or anything, since I was three grades behind him and obviously not a threat. After all, if he really cared about her, I was sure he would not intentionally do something to make her sad. I was so naïve!

But then one day he wanted to walk me home from school. I discouraged him by saying that my mother would not approve. He offered to take my books.

"No, I am quite capable of carrying my own books," I told him.

But he was not one to give up. In order to dissuade him, I brought his girlfriend into the conversation.

"How would she feel if she knew that you wanted to walk home with me?" I asked.

"Let me worry about her," he said. So I did. I asked him to start on his way home only after he had walked me almost home.

We continued to talk at school, but I wondered, at age thirteen, what a junior classman wanted with this very innocent teenager. Despite our growing friendship, was he really one of the boys my mother often warned me about? I was bound to find out for myself. He was very intelligent, self-centered, and ambitious. Each day during his paper route, he would pass by the house, hoping to see me outside. Sometimes he was lucky, sometimes not. I learned of this, years after we became adults.

My worst nightmare came true one day: While walking to my third period class, I was confronted by his girlfriend. She was visibly upset and made no excuses for it.

"You need to leave my man alone," she demanded. "He belongs to me!"

I was offended. How dare she accuse me of trying to come between her and her boyfriend?

"You need to talk to *him* about that," I shot back. She had her nerve!

But not long after that encounter, and after many more conversations, I realized I was beginning to enjoy being around this boy more than I should, and he obviously felt the same way about me. I am sure that, at first, this had not been his intention. Nonetheless, clarification was needed.

I told him I did not wish to talk with him any longer. I did not appreciate his girlfriend speaking with me as she had. Something had to give. I was not going to be disrespected!

Thus I did not speak to him any longer; communication was cut off entirely.

As time passed, I enjoyed my freshman year, but I found I missed talking to him. Graduation for him was on the horizon, but he had impregnated a neighborhood girl—not his steady girl, either! This news made me sad; I expected better from him. I had no idea he would do such a thing. He *was* the kind of boy my mother had warned me about after all!

The following school year, as classes began, I focused more on my studies. I became friends with most of the guys in my class. They provided no threat. They all had girlfriends and would confide in me. I was not going steady with anybody, so it was easy for them to talk to me.

Once the girls understood that our relationships were purely platonic, my life became much easier at school. I enjoyed being by myself—after all, I was an only child and knew how to enjoy my own company.

One morning, during homeroom class, my girlfriend handed me an envelope. It was a letter from "him."

"Why is he writing to me?" I asked.

"Open it and read," she said. "You may find the answer."

I did find the answer on the five pages he had written. He apologized for his actions, for causing me to lose respect for him, and told me he thought of me constantly. I had thought of him too, but only in total confusion. I was not sure whether I should respond to the letter.

The following day, I was handed yet another letter. In fact, I received a letter every day that week, but I was certain I was not the only one getting letters from him; I wasn't that naïve anymore. I also received a letter every day the following week. I finally decided that I would answer him.

My mother found the letter that I had written in pieces in the wastebasket in my room. She confronted me, and I denied any emotional tie to him. She was not convinced that I was telling the truth, but I was not concerned about her doubt. I was almost 500 miles away from him, so it did not seem important.

And then a letter came that changed the way I related to him. We had created a bond that was not going to be broken, even though we were miles apart. It was not a physical bond, but an intellectual and emotional bond. He had become my dearest and closest friend. I knew nothing about infatuation, nor had I engaged in any illicit behavior; all I was certain of was my sadness when I could not talk to him.

Mother sensed danger and reacted accordingly. She forbade me to write to him, see him, or talk with him. I obeyed. He continued to write to me nonetheless.

CHAPTER 11

Teenage Frustrations

One of the most frustrating, embarrassing days of my life came on the morning that my stepfather accused me, without any proof, of disobeying my mother's wishes. After grilling me about the relationship as Mother stood silently by, he forced me into our car and drove to the young man's house.

I was not aware that the boy was at home on a visit from college. I sat in the car as my stepfather went into the house. I was not allowed to go inside. It seemed an eternity before he came out of the house.

"That boy said you had sex with him," he barked at me. I just looked at him in disbelief. I never said a word.

When we returned home, he related a story to my mother that I refused to believe. At that particular moment, I wondered what kind of man my mother had married. Was he insane or just mean? I knew what he was saying was not true.

Whether my stepfather had misunderstood, whether the young man had spoken truth, or whether he lied was not important to me; *I* knew the truth. I did not care what my stepfather believed. I felt in my heart that

Mother would never believe such a thing of her daughter; she knew better. We never spoke of it again; my mother did not like confrontations.

During my sophomore year in high school, desegregation became enforced in my state. And of course, my mother decided that since I was the child who started the issue of foreign students' right to attend school in the county, there was no reason for me to back down from this challenge.

I had no problem with her decision. After all, she was the mother, and I was the child. I missed the students with whom I had traveled on the path to education the previous ten years. But there was an untrod path I was destined to walk.

CHAPTER 12

A New Challenge

The first day of school at Dan McCarty High was quite different from that of Lincoln Park Academy. At this new school, I was in the presence of brand-new teachers, a much larger student body, and a new campus. But I was ready for the challenge!

When I entered my homeroom class that morning, I realized that, so far, I appeared to be the only one of eleven African American students who had come from Lincoln Park Academy as juniors in this class. I entered the class, offering a bright "good morning" in response to the scrutiny of my fellow classmates. Mr. Biedenharn, the homeroom teacher, said hello. I found it interesting that he called me by name. Obviously he had done his homework.

I took a vacant seat at one of the two long tables in the room and was relieved to see my cousin, Clifford, enter to sit across from me. He also had an expression of relief on his face. So we would be in this together—at least first thing in the morning.

The adjustment to classes and new teachers was relatively easy for me. I approached my classmates cautiously, letting them know that I was not

here to make life difficult for them, but to resume my high school education. As a result, they were friendly enough.

I enjoyed my classes, especially Mr. West's English class. He put a real
spin on everything he said. There was a pair of twin girls who sat in the
same aisle and across from me. A few days passed before I realized that I
was not looking at the same girl each day, they were so identical.

And then there was Ms. Wilkerson. She was very tough, but she brought
something to English literature that I had never experienced in an English
class before: respect for the written word. I had always liked grammar and
literature but never thought of endeavoring to respect it.

I made sure to sit in the very first seat at the front of the class so nothing
would distract me. This simple seat choice proved to be one of the best
decisions I made during that year. There were challenges during my junior
year that humbled and strengthened my character. They prepared me for
my senior year and last chance in high school. It was the launching pad for
my college career.

By now the school had grown accustomed to our faces and accepted
that desegregation would last. The student body was not unlike the rest
of the community; they soon learned that we were just ordinary teenagers
relating and behaving as teenagers do everywhere. We had problems and
issues to conquer just as everyone else did. Above all, we were individuals
in our own rights and not simply a group; we were individuals with our
own personalities and ways of relating and reacting.

As individuals, we approached diversity in a myriad of ways, according
to our individual family values. I don't recall any clashes of personality
due to my own family values, but instead I made a lot of unlikely friends.
I was engaging but not overwhelming. I took what was said to me with a
grain of salt, answered with warmth and sometimes tenacity, but always
respectfully and kindly. My only goal was to make the experience a positive
one and to leave Dan McCarty High School much more enlightened.

I finally reached the milestone of graduation day, and I was ready to face the world on my own for the very first time. Prior to this, my mother and stepfather always seemed to be simultaneously one step behind me and two steps ahead. Unlike most of my classmates, I was not sure I wanted to be too far away from home. I satisfied myself with the idea of going to private school for the first time, after knowing only public schools so far in my academic career. I decided to attend Oakwood College in Huntsville, Alabama, which certainly seemed a long way from home.

As the Greyhound bus pulled out of the terminal, I refused to look back for fear I would lose my resolve and get off at the next stop and return home. I willed myself to face forward; I knew I needed to see more of the world.

CHAPTER 13

On My Own

The first semester at college seemed to fly by. Before I knew it, I was back at school after my first Christmas break in 1967. I was not used to how much colder Huntsville could be compared to my native Florida. After class one morning, I hurried to climb my dormitory steps when I saw him walking across campus in my direction.

I wanted desperately to enter the warm building but hesitated as I thought I heard my name.

"Miss Baker," the man called anxiously.

I paused to let him catch up with me.

"Why, hello—it's Gabriel, isn't it?" I asked, noting that he shifted from leg to leg. I wasn't sure if he was nervous or if he was just trying to keep warm against the frosty bite of the wind, now at our backs. But in case he was nervous for some reason, I tried to put him at ease.

"You are Pierre Hunt's older brother aren't you?" I asked. I continued to make conversation, asking him how many years he had been at

Huntsville, but he did not seem interested in answering me. I tried another question as he opened the door to the dorm.

"How did you know my name?" I inquired.

"My brother," was his quiet reply.

I was anticipating the warmth of my room, and it showed on my face. He was taking much too long to say whatever was on his mind, and I, no longer the introverted teenaged girl I once was, wanted to help him say it.

"I really enjoy your brother's company," I said. "He was one of the very first young men I met on campus as I began my freshman year."

Strangely, the smile that I could see in his eyes never reached his lips. "Is that right, Miss Baker?" he asked. I wondered why my name sounded so different when he said it.

"So, what year is this for you?" I tried the question again.

He never really answered but instead said, "There is something that I wish to ask you, and I am not sure how to do it."

"Well, if you tell me what the question is, I will tell you how to ask me." I thought my remark was worth a smile. No such luck. Now I was done being patient and turned toward the inner steps leading to my room.

"There's a banquet coming up soon, and I would like to know if you would honor me by letting me escort you," he finally blurted.

I'd heard rumors that he was engaged to be married after his graduation from college, whenever that would be, since he never answered my inquiry as to when his graduation would take place. I wondered if I was just part of the new crop of girls on campus and considered fair game for the upperclassmen.

"Aren't you getting married soon?" I asked.

His answer came much faster than I expected. "Yes, I am," he said. He looked in my eyes as he spoke, but I felt as if he could see right through to my soul. By this time, we had taken a seat on the last step of the landing. I was glad I was sitting—the sensation was so strange, I'm not sure I wouldn't have fallen. I told him that I would have to do some serious thinking about his invitation and would get back to him. He seemed pleased that I did not say no. Pressing his advantage, he asked if I would have dinner with him the next evening. I cautiously nodded *yes* and turned to go upstairs.

The first thing I did after gaining my composure was to get to a vacant telephone in the hall. I needed more information about this engaging and handsome young man, and who better to ask than his brother?

"Pierre, I need to see you sometime today if possible. There is something I need to talk with you about," I said into the phone.

Pierre had become like a surrogate brother to me; I felt very comfortable talking with him. He had a serious girlfriend in another state, and he made no secret about his feelings for her; I considered him a safe, handsome, personable, hazel-eyed devil. I enjoyed my talks with him and appreciated his brotherly advice.

Once I discovered that his brother, Gabriel, was indeed engaged to be married after graduation in June, I felt quite safe in sitting with him at dinner. After all, he was only looking for a dinner companion, and had chosen me, for whatever reason. Even though his brother had informed me of his pending marriage, I wanted the news from the source, and brought it up at dinner.

"So, I hear that you are getting married after graduation," I said.

"That's the plan," he answered.

"Congratulations," I told him. "I hope that marriage is all that you expect it to be." My eyes never left his face; I wanted to know if he was as sincere as he had first appeared. "Where is your fiancée right now?"

He had a moment to contemplate his answer as one of his roommates greeted him while joining us at the table. "This is Miss Rose Baker," he said.

I acknowledged the introduction but remained focused on his face in expectation of the answer to my question.

"Her name is Mary," he said, "and she lives in Buffalo, New York. She wants to get married right after graduation." He had a noncommittal look in his eyes.

When I am engaged, I thought, *I sure want my man to be more excited than this man seems to be.*

After dinner, we took a short walk before I had to be in the dormitory. He asked if I would eat breakfast with him the following morning. I had not planned to come down for breakfast, but he persuaded me by reminding me that my body was indeed the temple of God, and should be nourished. Who was I to argue with that logic?

CHAPTER 14

Here's to Friendship

Gabriel and I became fast friends. I was frustrated with the immaturity of most of the young men on campus who seemed interested in wooing me. It was so refreshing to be with someone who understood my ideals, dreams, and goals while never seeming inclined to take advantage of my youthful naïveté.

Gabriel, unlike the other men on campus, did not seem to care whether my hair was long or short, whether my clothing matched or not, whether I played the piano or not. And I was tired of hearing how pretty and well-dressed I was. How I walked with poise and grace. How well-spoken I was. It had all gotten old.

So I welcomed his sincere interest in the natural course of life. He appreciated my maturity. I appreciated his love for God and his family. I suppose that is why it took me so long before I realized that he had become enamored with me, and I with him.

One Saturday afternoon, as I awaited his return from visiting the local prison where he spoke with prisoners regarding their relationship with their Maker, he approached me where I sat under one of the many oak trees on campus. His whole face seemed to light up. I watched his face and thought what a lucky woman Mary would be to have him as her husband. Something in my face must have alerted Gabriel that something was wrong because he gave me a strange look in return. At that moment, I realized the happiness I had once felt for him and his ensuing marriage was now gone, and I had no idea how to deal with this new feeling. He was of no help as he looked into my eyes, telling me how he wished that I had been there with him. When he pleaded with me to go with him on the next visit to the prison, I promised him I would.

We spent many more days under that oak tree getting to know each other. Gabriel and I soon confided in one another things that had happened in our lives that no one else knew about. I was flattered he would trust me that much. He cleared up many misconceptions I had adopted about relationships. I soon learned I could trust him and believe what he told me; he had given me no reason to think otherwise.

The time for the banquet was fast approaching, and I had no idea what I would wear. Gabriel kept asking what color I was wearing, but I had not chosen anything. I had to work fast. I called my mother, and she said that she would make me a baby-blue gown. My mother made everything I wore, so I knew that all would be well. She had exactly three weeks in which to sew the gown, find shoes and a purse to match, and mail them to me in time for the banquet. When I think back, I realize Gabriel never told me why his fiancée was not going to be his date. I never asked, and we never spoke of it.

When I told my mother about my friendship with Gabriel, she did not seem concerned that he was engaged to be married. She always said, "God has a plan for your life, Rose Ann, and He alone knows what that is. Never thwart the will of God! Continue to hold onto your principles, love the Lord with all your heart, be obedient to His will, and you will reap the harvest." I have never forgotten that telephone call nor her final words at the end of that conversation: "He knows that he is engaged."

The night of the banquet, Gabriel came to the dorm for me, white floral box in hand. In it was the most magnificent double white orchid I had ever laid eyes on. He pinned it on my shoulder and looked deeply into my eyes as he spoke.

"You are more beautiful than I ever imagined you could be," he said.

I wasn't sure whether that was a compliment, but his look told me that he appreciated what he saw.

The photo we took that night said it all. People who later saw it wondered why I didn't comprehend his feelings for me. They claimed it was obvious in the way he looked at me. I was in denial; he was in love with another woman. He would be married in five months. He was just my very best friend. I did not want to mess that up. He was graduating and would be gone from my life forever.

It was his baby sister who informed me that she thought her brother "Gabby" liked me. I told her that I was sure that he did, as a friend. She gave me "that look" and went away. I was confused as ever after that encounter. Why would she tell me such a thing? I had to find out more, but I was afraid to ask.

Gabriel and I became inseparable after that banquet. He would wait for me in the mornings to walk with me to class. He would send up breakfast for me if I did not make it to the cafeteria on time. He sought me out on campus in order to spend as much time as possible getting to know me, and I him. We shared stories of our childhood. We spoke of situations we endured and conquered. His soft-spoken manner endeared him to me.

I often visited him as he worked in the music building, where he first discovered that I played the piano. I was in one of the practice rooms entertaining myself until he was done with work. I was well into my favorite rendition of *How Great Thou Art* when I felt a presence in the room. I turned quickly and almost knocked into Gabriel. He stood directly behind the bench.

"Why did you not tell me that you played?" he asked.

"I was hiding this talent from the ministerial students," was my answer.

His eyes smiled in amusement. "I am glad that you now share this secret with me," he said. "And by the way, this is one of my favorite songs."

He sat down next to me and asked that I finish the hymn. Whenever I hear that melody or the words, "Then sings my soul . . . how great thou art," I think of sharing it with Gabriel.

CHAPTER 15

Love Found, Love Lost

As Gabriel's graduation approached, my anxiety grew. The thought of not having him around to confide in any longer weighed heavily, yet I knew that God indeed had a plan for my life, and I would trust His leading. It was not until the morning of graduation that I got an inkling of what that plan might be.

Gabriel's mother had come for the ceremonies, and I was finally introduced to her. She was a lot like her son—soft-spoken, unassuming, and very personable. She had the most beautiful, piercing eyes. She seemed to take a liking to me from the very start, as I did to her. She was very easy to talk with.

"I think my Gabby likes you very much," she quietly told me after our second meeting. "But his fiancée is here."

"Isn't he getting married?" I asked.

"We will see," she answered. "We will see."

I had not planned to stay for the graduation ceremony, even though I wanted to say my final goodbyes to friends in the class. But Gabriel had begged me to stay. He convinced me that he needed to speak with me after the ceremonies and did not have the time to do so at that moment.

Gabriel's older sister introduced me to Mary, his fiancée. Mary eyed me suspiciously as I extended my hand in greeting. I, on the one hand, felt like I was on exhibition. On the other hand, I felt relieved that I had finally met her. I wasn't worried!

Graduation went off without a hitch, and Gabriel sought me out after the ceremony.

"I will be coming down to Florida this summer, on my way to the Bahamas. Would it be all right for me to call you?"

Even though I was a bit confused, I quickly answered, "Why, yes, of course!"

He planted a kiss on my cheek, gave me an awfully long hug, and disappeared.

I went to the dormitory, collected my bags, and took a taxi to the terminal. I wondered why I felt such a lump in my throat as I boarded the bus with other students. It was a very long ride home.

Once at home, I prepared my parents for the possibility of Gabriel's visit. He would stay at a relative's house for the short time that he would be in town. I was very much surprised by the butterflies in my mid-section and could not contain my excitement.

The day arrived, and I met him at the airport. Gabriel and I had spoken by telephone almost every day since I last saw him. It seemed a bit strange at the time, especially since I had misgivings about his canceled wedding plans. I could not wait to find out what had really happened.

Gabriel spent only three days with my family and me before he had to leave for the Bahamas; he had been invited to spend a week with his best friend. I was sad to see him go, but he promised to come back on his way home after his trip.

While Gabriel soaked up the sun in Nassau with his friends, I was feeling very confused. My parents had taken immediately to Gabriel and only complicated matters by constantly reminding me what a fantastic young man he was. It certainly hadn't taken him long to make an impression.

My mother seemed to be mesmerized by his sharp, cool, good looks. "He looks at a person as if he could see through to their very soul," she kept saying. As if I did not have a clue as to what she was talking about, I would look at her and smile, though I was pleased that she liked him.

But on the other hand, I knew I had to change my parents' minds about any thoughts of him and me together. It would never work, I kept telling myself. He could never justify leaving his fiancée literally at the altar, for that is what he said he had done. But what I didn't know was that Gabriel had secretly spoken to my mother regarding his long-range plans for the future. And after much convincing on his part, he told her that I was the woman with whom he wished to spend the rest of his life. In reply, my mother had given him a list of things that he had to accomplish before he could have her blessing. She wanted to make sure that he could afford me. The strict West Indian cultural influence rose up within her in a magnificent way.

When Gabriel returned from Nassau, we spent an evening together on my front lawn.

"My most precious pearl of greatest price," he declared, "when Jesus comes back to earth to claim His own, I want you standing beside me so that we may enter heaven together as man and wife. Will you make this dream come true for me?"

My confusion changed to shock! I looked down at him from my chair, moonlight shining on that well-chiseled countenance of his, and was speechless. It took some time before I was able to respond with, "I need some time to think."

He had already gotten the answer he needed from my mother, so he really wasn't worried. I left him outside and rushed into the house to ask my mother how she felt about having Gabriel as a son-in-law. The poor guy was outside all alone in the moonlight while I pondered the right way to answer.

"I know how you feel about him," said Mother. "You need to tell him *yes*."

I had my answer, and turned to go back to where Gabriel waited.

"As long as you wait until you get your degree," she called after me, but I was already out the door.

Gabriel left for New York the following day, promising to call me when he arrived home. It was a bittersweet farewell.

CHAPTER 16

A Final Farewell

On a particularly chilly evening, I was in my dorm room studying for exams when I heard the sound of my own name over the intercom, summoning me for a telephone call at the end of the hall. I hurried to the phone and heard Gabriel's voice on the other end. I missed him so much as I began my sophomore year so far away from him, and his voice reminded me of the ache in my heart.

"Darling," he began. "I have bad news." His mother was not recuperating as expected from major surgery. I could hear the pain in his voice as he spoke. My heart reached out to him over the distance as I now shared his pain. He paused after telling me the news, as if there was something else he wanted to say, but could not. "I wish that you could be here with me," he was finally able to mutter.

I knew that I would have to get my mother's permission as well as that of the Dean of Women before beginning a response to that statement. So instead I asked him, "Do you want me to come?"

"I don't think that she will last much longer," he said.

"I'll make the necessary arrangements and call you back in an hour."

After the conversation with Gabriel, I telephoned my parents to ask for permission and financial assistance to go to New York. I was met with resistance. My all-wise mother said that she would think about it and call me later. She was reluctant, even though the prognosis was dim for Gabriel's mom. I was confused. Mother was a very compassionate and loving woman. What was wrong? It seemed she was afraid for us, Gabriel and me. I was still a teenager, she reminded me. Gabriel was an experienced, mature man. We loved each other. Things could happen unexpectedly when someone was experiencing the terminal illness of a loved one, especially a mother. To me it did not seem a good time for this lecture.

When the conversation ended, I knew that she would not call me back. I knew she believed that even though she did not say no outright, I would not be comfortable going without her permission. I had learned important lessons of obedience early in life, and now was not the time to regress. Nevertheless, I began packing for the trip.

Gabriel called back before the hour was up. His mom had taken a turn for the worse, and he needed me. Would I come? I couldn't possibly tell him no. I told him that I would be on the next flight out of Huntsville. In the interim, I asked my dean to intervene. I could not wait for my mother's call; I would just suffer any consequences later.

I prayed as the plane ascended into the night sky en route to La Guardia that the Lord would forgive me for what I needed to do. Surely Mother would understand. She could not be everywhere to protect me. She would have to trust me enough to do what was right. I settled into my seat, hoping that I would arrive on time to say my goodbyes.

When we landed, snow blew from the sky like a white hurricane. I had never seen so much snow all at once. It was cold and miserable, but as Gabriel met my glance in the distance, I became warmer than a bear in its cave during hibernation. I was so relieved to see him. All I could think was how much I loved him.

My poor, sad baby! Gabriel brought me up to speed on his mom's desperate fight for life, nearing its final outcome. My future husband needed me; he was happy at least that I was there. Mom Hunt passed away shortly after I arrived at the house. My own life would never be the same from that night forward.

And just for the record, my mother was right. I was tempted almost past what I could handle. Gabriel was so grief-stricken that when he held on to me during the next few days, I could feel his heart breaking. I wanted to wrap him up in my love and never let him go, to give him every part of me in comfort, but I knew I couldn't—not yet. I did what I could to let him know that I would always be there to love him for the rest of our lives, and that had to be enough.

It was.

CHAPTER 17

Making Difficult Decisions

Aftergoo much discussion and counsel from an older brother, Gabriel and I moved up our wedding plans to accommodate living arrangements for his baby brother. We would get married at the end of the following summer, and his brother, who needed to finish high school, would be with us.

After the discussion among the siblings ended in no concrete resolution, I was surprised that no one wanted to take responsibility for the baby brother. Surely one of those living in the area would allow him to at least stay with them until his final year of high school was completed. But it was I who offered the out for which the family seemed to be looking.

I knew that my mother would offer to take him under her wing without hesitation; she was that kind of person. I felt so terrible for Enacio. When I presented my solution to Gabby, he hesitated before answering. "What school will he attend? He doesn't know anyone in Florida, and you will be back in Alabama finishing your studies."

What a predicament. Finally, I agreed to push our wedding date ahead so that Enacio could finish high school while being near to family on whom he could depend. The patriarch of the family had no input because he did not come to America when his wife and children migrated years prior. Therefore, Enacio had nowhere to go.

We were married in my hometown following my sophomore year. It was a long-distance courtship, but I was never too lonely. I was still in school, and Gabriel's sister and brother were there to look after me in his absence. His sister became my roommate.

On the day we were married, August 17, 1969, I knew in my heart that ours was a love that would last forever—"Until death would we part." When he discovered that I took my virginity with me to our marriage bed, he knelt beside the bed and thanked God for giving me to him. I was moved beyond measure and loved him even more than I thought possible.

We settled into married life. It had all the challenges of most marriages, but we always put God first and never went to bed angry. My husband was not a man of many words; I, on the other hand, was a woman of *lots* of words. We complimented each other in a way that seemed strange to some of our friends. I always made sure that he felt loved, even when I was displeased with something he said or did. In later years, our children never heard us argue. They were reprimanded with love and tenderness.

Our first child was born at Kings County Hospital, Brooklyn, New York. She was the most beautiful, precious, little bundle of delight we could have ever imagined. I had no idea that I could love anyone as much as I loved my new baby girl.

My parents had come up from Florida to be present at her birth. My due date was June 28. However, after a week of walking me up and down Fifth Avenue, they had to leave. It was July 6, and I went into labor that very night! Ramona presented herself to the world the day after they had left for home. She was named in honor of my father and Gabriel's oldest brother, who both bore the name of Raymond.

Gabriel took to fatherhood right away, changing diapers, bathing and soothing his baby. He was a natural. And since I had so much experience taking care of my neighbors' babies, it was a breeze for me to manage motherhood along with my other responsibilities. We loved our new role as parents.

Four weeks after the birth of our little girl, I traveled with her to Florida. Gabriel and I had both been accepted at the University of Miami to continue further educational goals. We needed to find living accommodations, settle in, and be ready for school in September. The baby and I went ahead by plane, and Gabriel would follow in a couple of weeks with his little brother.

My parents met us at the airport. They were so excited to see their first grandchild. From the moment I handed Ramona over to her grandmother and said, "Here you go, Mother, your granddaughter is finally here," I felt like a stepchild. The only time I was able to hold my baby was to breastfeed her. I didn't complain, though; I needed the rest and welcomed the help. Ramona was a very good baby. She was happy and alert, and seldom cried. She had me or her grandparents to meet her every need, and she flourished into a well-adjusted baby.

When her father finally came to Florida, we left my parents' house and moved to the campus apartments at the University of Miami. I enrolled in classes, found work at Mercy Hospital, and Gabriel and I began our new life as parents, students, and providers for our family. Gabriel's younger brother enrolled to finish his senior year at Coral Gables High School.

I would take my baby to classes with me. After classes, I would rush home, get ready for work, get her settled with my neighbor, and walk to the bus stop. I worked every day from 3:00 p.m. to 11:00 p.m. and on alternate weekends. We were all exhausted.

Ramona did not take well to being left with my neighbor for three hours every day. Enacio would watch her once he got home at 3:00 p.m., but Gabriel soon decided that we had to make other arrangements. My parents were overjoyed when we chose to let them watch her for us. They were two hours away, but they were our only choice, since we were both in school—and particularly because we'd made the decision that our children would not have baby-sitters unless they were close family members. Furthermore, Enacio needed time for himself. It was not fair to burden him with the responsibility, even though he never complained. We missed our baby terribly, but we knew that she was in a good place. It was a bittersweet sacrifice for the next three months, but we made it. On my days off, I would travel the two hours to be with my baby.

CHAPTER 18

A New Addition

By this time, we were pregnant with our second child. Gabriel and I had talked about the number of children we would have long before we were married. I had informed him that I wished to have all four children before I was twenty-five years of age or I would have none. I realized that sacrifices would have to be made, and I was willing to make them. He reluctantly agreed. What other choice did he have since I would be the one carrying them? So we were headed for number two.

Geno entered the world eleven hours before his father's twenty-seventh birthday, and Gabriel was overjoyed at his birthday present. He had his Gabriel Eugene, Jr. He was perfect, except for those blue eyes. Thank God they turned light brown after awhile! I was worried at first. He was dark-complexioned, and blue eyes did not go well with that skin. The nurses on the floor could not get enough of him; he was quite the charmer from the very beginning. Gabriel and I were in love all over again. We now had two of the most precious darlings imaginable!

His older sister was so curious about her new baby brother. She was only fifteen months old and just beginning to form two syllable words. She immediately dubbed him "G-Boy," and her brother carried this nickname until he was almost two years old.

Later, his preschool teacher, Judy, shortened his middle name, Eugene, to "Geno," which is the name he's still affectionately called by everyone who knows him.

We traveled to Berrien Springs, Michigan to Andrews University the following term after our son's birth. It was there that I gave birth to our third and final child. Leonel was named for his paternal grandfather, Leonel. He made his way into the world very early before his due date. Prematurely born, he was not a pretty sight. I was afraid to hold him. My other babies were born plump and round and filled out. This little boy was long, shriveled, and hungry.

But Gabriel was in love at first sight all over again. There was something about Leonel that endeared him immediately to his father. They developed a different kind of bond from the moment he caught him from my womb. It was a good thing; I was at a loss as to what to do at first, though he had a face to die for; he was his father's double.

When Leonel was six months old, Gabriel and I talked about having that fourth child and agreed that we would begin the process. It was the night that I found out my dear, sweet husband had applied for and been accepted to the Ph.D.-M.D. program at Loma Linda University in California.

I was happy because he was ecstatic; we were going to celebrate, but then it occurred to me that I did not want to be pregnant three thousand miles away from any family while he was studying. That thought alone brought cold reality to my brain, and there was no baby-making that night!

The following morning, I began planning the strategy for our next undertaking. I was not a happy camper as I finished the details of our packing, realizing that our plans had taken yet another turn in the opposite direction. But I knew that my husband needed my love and support in this different endeavor. Loving him and our family was what I did best.

CHAPTER 19

New Changes

We focused on making the move to California instead of Florida, where Gabriel had promised that he wanted to settle down. As far as I was concerned, our family was complete, minus number four.

I did not have to hear the words "I love you" every day. I knew and felt my husband's love in many different ways. I could walk into a crowded room and his love for me would fill the entire place. He would gaze into my eyes and I would immediately know what was in his heart. His appreciation for my parenting and culinary skills were obvious whenever he complimented me by bringing strangers to the house for dinner.

Gabriel took every opportunity to make me feel his love. He complimented me on being a good wife and mother to "his" children. Even during his absences from us, the children and I could feel his love covering us like a warm, toasty, blanket on a bitter winter's night.

The challenges we faced as a couple brought us closer to God and to each other. His good-natured charm and quiet good looks brought unsolicited attention from the opposite sex. It kept me on my knees.

One young lady in particular presented a minor problem. She courted his attention, even though she was aware of his marital status. She befriended his family in order to get closer to him. It worked, yet she had no idea that I was aware of her infatuation with my husband.

Consequently, she became adept at finding excuses to be near him. She came to the house quite frequently to have dinner. She wrote letters to me as well as to my husband. It was by no coincidence that she made it to the same institution to study medicine. I am sure that coincidences happen, but I was not naïve enough to believe this one. I never mentioned this to anyone. There was no threat to my family involved in her matriculation at Loma Linda. So she became one of my "best" friends; I am sure she still thinks she got one over on me because I never mentioned anything to her or my Gabriel.

She went as far as attempting suicide when he became ill. There may have been other mitigating circumstances, but I think it was pure guilt that led her to the sad decision to end her life. I was not angry; she needed the attention, but I had his attention, and his children had his attention. If there was any left, she was welcome to it. He had that effect on everyone. When he spoke to you, he could make you feel that you were the only person in the world at the time, and at this time, his wife and children were his world.

I made sure that Gabriel saw her and had a chance to speak with her regarding her suicide attempt. I drove him to the institution in another city for a visit. She was in bad shape. I loved him beyond measure, and I pitied her. We never spoke of that night. Wherever she is right now, I hope she has found peace within. I did find out that she got married the year my husband died.

CHAPTER 20

Staying Strong in the Face of a Storm

I t was April 1, 1977, April Fool's Day. Even though I had worked hard all day and the kids were tucked safely in bed, I could not settle down to fall asleep. I had the peculiar feeling that something was terribly wrong. After tossing and turning, I finally dozed off at around 11:00 p.m. It was not a restful sleep as my mind was still wandering.

I was awakened by Gabriel's touch when he arrived home from work at the Medical Center. I sat up in bed to talk to him as I usually did. He sat down on my side of the bed and held my hands in his. And then my world fell apart.

"Lil' Mother," he said, "the blood work that I performed on myself tonight was not good. My white count was so very high that it could not be read on the machine."

"What do you mean it was so high?" I asked. I needed an explanation.

"I have leukemia," he blurted out.

I knew enough about the disease to know that there was no known cure. Because it was April 1, I thought that he was playing a very sick April Fool's joke on me. I let him know that I did not appreciate his humor.

When I turned on the bedside lamp and looked at his face, I realized it was no joke. He took me in his arms as he told me there would be a bone marrow test done the following morning to confirm his self-diagnosis. I could feel his whole body shaking as he held onto me. I was in a state of shock and could not react to what I was hearing.

After some time, I backed out of his arms, stood up, and in disbelief, cried, "But you can't die, you just can't! We have so much living to do, Gabby."

"I know, Lil' Mother. Our children need their father. I don't want to leave them. We will be alright. God is still in charge."

I telephoned to give my parents the news and to ask them to pray for us. We fell asleep in each other's arms as we did every night.

The following morning, the children and I went to church as their uncle took their father to the hospital for the bone marrow test. I prayed that God would give us the strength to do what we had to do. I kept hoping the blood tests were all wrong, even though Gabriel had informed me that it had been run more than twice.

Anticipation was making me more nervous as the minutes passed. When I finally got the results from the test, I was devastated. The children went up to the hospital to see their father. Dr. Robert Rentschler was the oncologist who explained to us what our expectations should be.

I listened with my ears, but my heart broke with each syllable he spoke. The man I shared my life with was going to die soon. My children would be without a father. My most trusted friend would soon be gone. What was I to do without him?

Reality called me into the present because my children were hungry for lunch. How would I explain all of this to them? I sent them down to the cafeteria with their uncle while I took the time to digest the news and help my husband get settled in his hospital bed. He would begin treatment right away. There was no time to lose. I left after awhile to bring toiletries and pajamas from home. I did not want my husband to see me fall apart. I needed some time alone, away from the hospital, so I was relieved that I had to run the errand.

My mother came out from Florida to spend some time with us. She would sit with Gabby for hours at the hospital so I could have time to deal with work, negotiate the children's schedules, and keep house. She was a most comforting presence for us all, though I would not learn the real significance of her visit for years to come.

The following summer, we took the children to Florida, as was our custom, to spend our vacation with my parents. My mother looked forward to having her grandchildren for the entire season. I had them enrolled in recreation activities each summer: tennis, swimming, gymnastics, and music camps to keep them busy and help them learn new things.

Once we got the children settled into their routine, Gabby and I boarded a plane for his native home, St. Martin in the French Antilles. It would be a couple of weeks together for us to enjoy some alone time while digesting his fate. We had not seen his father and brother, who resided on this island, for some time. It was a bittersweet reunion. One day, Gabby felt good enough to take a picnic basket along with us as we waded to the little Cay, not far from his brother's home. The picnic basket we took along came in handy as we worked up an appetite. We caught fish and threw them back into the ocean. We talked about what the distant future could hold for me and the children. We reminisced about how we met, our times at Oakwood College. We laughed at how afraid of heights he was and how he would not join the children on any rides at Disney, which included being up high.

At other moments, we listened to the sound of our own hearts beating as we watched the waves come and go on the shore. This went on for hours before we noticed the rising tide and had to head home. It was the most wonderful day ever and yet one of the worst days of my life. And I had the sunburn from hell to prove it. It took all the strength I had to hold back the torrent of tears I felt gathering behind my eyes.

My husband was beginning to look like himself again. We had periodically checked his blood count and were pleased with the results. His mustache had begun to grow back in; there was almost an occasional smile. But my gut told me that this was merely the calm before the real storm. I kept this revelation to myself.

The time we spent in St. Martin was bittersweet, for we knew that this would be the last trip home for Gabby. The smell of the ocean, coupled with the familiar faces in Cul de Sac, brought him a tremendous amount of pleasure. He passed that feeling along to me as we lay in each other's arms one evening.

The scene at the airport when we said our final good-byes to the family was filled with an indescribable intensity of emotion. We were so sad to leave everyone but had to get back to the children and the reality of Gabby's illness. Our children were so happy to see us when we returned to Miami International. We would spend another week in Florida before going back home to Loma Linda.

The Lincoln Park Academy Class of '67 was celebrating its tenth reunion, and I was invited to the activities. Gabby did not want me to miss the event and encouraged me to make an appearance alone since he was not up to meeting strangers; we had just returned from our trip the previous day.

The celebration offered me the opportunity to socialize with some of my classmates. I welcomed the chance to think about other things, if only for an hour. It gave Gabby time to rest up for the long plane ride back home. It also gave him some alone time with one of the other women in his life, my mother. The bond between them was unbreakable. She loved him as if she had brought him into the world herself, and he loved her deeply in return.

At last, we finally arrived back at home, our home together where we truly believed we belonged now, and were ready to resume what was left of life as we knew it. The more Gabby grew to look like his old self, the more anxious I became. I did not want to let him know what I was thinking, so I pretended to be hopeful.

Some of my acquaintances accused me of being pessimistic because I voiced my concerns to them. Instead of offering a listening ear to my suffering, they passed judgment on my emotions. I had dealt with death and dying my entire lifetime. I was not afraid to face the reality of death when my loved ones surrendered to it. If there was a long illness involved, I learned early to recognize the many stages of mortality. My life had prepared me for Gabby's illness, and so I turned a deaf ear to the judgmental opinions and focused on loving my husband while I still had him.

I went back to work with a heavy but determined mind. The children and my coworkers were happy to see me and their playmates. Ramona was now in first grade. Geno and Lele were at the Children's Center with me. I continued to keep their schedules as closely as possible. Gabby decided that he wanted to continue the research he was doing for his Ph.D. I was ambivalent to this idea but allowed him his freedom to choose what he thought best. I could tell that he was wrestling with his mortality.

One evening, as we lay in bed talking, my beloved husband turned to me and said he wanted to have that fourth child we talked about early in our marriage. I turned more closely to him as I questioned, "Are you kidding me?" I was immediately caught off guard by the pleading in his eyes.

"I know that you would be left alone with a young baby, but I really want to do this! You remember that we had chosen her name years ago after Leonel was born."

I thought that the chemo and radiation had affected his brain in a very unique way.

"So you want to have little Desiree, and leave me with four children instead of three?" There was never any question that it would be another girl. We were so proficient at predicting what sex each child would be during my pregnancy that there was no doubt. "You have lost your ever-loving mind," I whispered slowly and deliberately to him. "You want to leave me with a tangible memory of your illness? How selfish could you be, Gabby?" I was ashamed of my words the minute they left my mouth, but did not apologize.

Later that night, as I lay in his arms, my husband explained why he wanted me to have another child. He really thought that I was disappointed on the night we planned to conceive, back at Andrews University. I was, but the disappointment only lasted for a night. I had long gotten over it! My love for children was satisfied with the three we conceived, and those with whom I worked. I told him I had been satisfied having sex without the consequences for four years now and asked him why I would mess that up. Gabby laughed out loud at that revelation. I never heard him laugh that way again.

I worried every day as I waved goodbye to him when he traveled the sidewalk to the hospital laboratory. He was not fooling me one bit. I knew that he felt tired and weak. I knew that his heart was heavy. I knew that God was preparing us for the final countdown. I promised myself to be ready. It was a promise I could not keep.

CHAPTER 21

The Approaching Storm

Shortly after we settled back into our routine as a family, Gabby's white count accelerated at a very fast rate. It was September, the week after Labor Day. As he looked at me with those beautiful, piercing eyes of his, holding my hands, I realized that my greatest nightmare was now a reality. He had to go back to the hospital and start another round of chemotherapy and radiation.

I felt as if the very bottom of my soul had fallen way down into a very deep, dark, abyss, someplace where I could not retrieve it. I felt myself falling along with my soul and had to hold onto my beloved husband with all my strength in order to stay on *terra firma* with him.

I was not sad; I was so much more than sad—I was angry! So very angry! I had felt this anger many times before, only this time, the rage I felt was overwhelming. I couldn't breathe. I couldn't focus. I couldn't cry. I couldn't talk. All I felt was an all-consuming wrath. There was nothing that even Gabby could do to reach me. I had fallen headlong into that abyss, and only by surrendering to God would I be brought out.

That evening, we told our babies that Daddy had to go back to the hospital in the morning. But Daddy was looking so well these days, and I saw the disbelief in their eyes.

"But why?" they asked innocently.

"I need more medicine," Daddy replied.

Our littlest one guardedly asked the next question: "Why can't you take your medicine at home? Then you won't have to go back to the hospital."

Daddy was not getting off that easily. Leonel had a way of making a person answer his questions to his satisfaction. But instead of answering, Gabby turned his head in my direction, as if the question was specifically directed at me.

"The doctor won't let us bring the medicine home."

I thought this answer was brilliant until the oldest, Ramona, offered her solution. "All you have to do is ask, Mommy," she said to me. She still believed her mommy had the solution for any problem.

It was now time for the middle child to contribute. Geno stepped up to look his daddy right in the eyes. "I'll ask the doctor, Daddy," he offered. "He won't say no to me. I would even make sure that you take all of the medicine before we go to school. And when we come back from school, I would give you some more of your medicine." Geno was sure that he had come up with the right solution.

"Please, Mommy, can you make Daddy stay home with us and take his medicine?" they continued to ask; after all, mommies are supposed to fix everything. This I couldn't fix. I made my best attempt to convince our babies that Daddy would only have to stay for a little while. We could see him every day and night. We could even spend the night sometimes. They did not see me cross my fingers behind me as I struggled to placate them.

It seemed they either accepted my statement or were thinking up more questions as they finally all hung their heads and walked away from us, taking shelter in their separate bedrooms. I made no move to follow them.

When my husband took me in his arms much later that evening, we held onto each other as if we were on a sinking ship without life jackets, knowing that tomorrow would never come for us again. That night gave us a much-needed opportunity to talk about the future—as if we had any, I thought. What in the world was I going to do without my soul mate?

Morning light hit the two of us, still entwined in each other's arms. We reluctantly rose from bed and dropped Ramona off at school together, down the hill from Loma Linda's campus. Gabby and I parked the car and walked the boys to their classrooms at the Children's Center before going up the sidewalk to the hospital. It was a silent walk. We had used our bodies and our words to say all we could say the previous night.

Dr. Rentschler had prepared orders for Gabby, and his treatments resumed that afternoon. We attempted to make light of the fact that he was just beginning to have hair again (meaning his mustache and beard). After spending time getting him settled and as comfortable as possible under the circumstances, I made my way down the hall to the elevators, to the chapel.

It was here that I poured out my heart to God. It was here that I found the courage to ask why, how, when, where? None of this made any sense to me. Gabby and I had only just begun, and now we were fast reaching our end.

"Give me strength, Lord, to make it through the changes in our lives," I prayed. "Help me to be the wife and mother that I must be in this, our hour of trial. Keep your loving arms of love and protection continually around our babies. They do not understand why their daddy is not going to be around to do the things to which they have grown accustomed. No more walks in the park to feed the ducks, no more visits to the beach to watch the seagulls, no more Saturday afternoon visits to Forest Falls, no more trips to Disney or the San Diego Zoo or Magic Mountain or Knottsberry Farm."

I felt as if my whole body would disintegrate if I stayed one moment longer in this quiet place where I could hear my own heart beating. What was God thinking? Surely this was not His idea! I needed to talk with Him another time about this, but not now.

I was not aware of the time as I drove away from the hospital. The long drive to nowhere in particular took me hours. I drove to Yucaipa and knelt beside the sand statue of the Savior, hoping to gain some clarity. This place had become one of our favorite places to visit on Saturday afternoons. I turned my attention to the open tomb, which was not yet completed, and felt a wave of emotion sweep over me. My gaze soon took in the three crosses on the hill.

"Lord, thank you for giving your life for me," I sobbed. "Help me to be grateful for all that you have done. Sometimes the load gets heavy, and I forget momentarily that you are there to lighten my burden, not take it away. I want to accept this challenge that you have placed before me, but I don't know where to begin. Would you help me?"

I left with renewed strength to make it through whatever came my way.

Were it not for Dr. Wilbur Alexander, head chaplain at the Medical Center, the following months would have been disastrous. He was so sympathetic to the many changes I was experiencing. He helped me to maintain my equilibrium when I took too much pleasure in blaming God for testing me.

I was furious with God for a very long time and was not afraid to let Him know. We had developed that kind of relationship over the years. When I did something that He wasn't too keen on, He let me know. When He allowed the devil to tempt me, I let Him know that I did not like it.

We were good friends, God and I. We often had seriously hot discussions. He let me rant and rave. He reprimanded accordingly. But like the friends we were, we always made up. After all, He always had the upper hand and always won the argument.

CHAPTER 22

Grieving Children

One day in November, I received news that my oldest son, who was five years old at the time, was missing from school. How could he be missing? I was having some problems with one of my sisters-in-law at the time and thought that perhaps she had taken him. She had threatened to take all of our children to another state. I became understandably worried for more than one reason as I headed for the school.

"Okay, Lord, what are you and the devil up to now?" I muttered.

The school had searched everywhere on campus for Geno without success. I was trying not to panic. Surely he was just playing hide-and-seek someplace, waiting to be discovered. This was not the case. When we found him attempting to walk to Florida, I knew that it was time for things to change. He was not handling his daddy's illness very well and said that he wanted to go to Florida to be with his Grammy until Daddy was better.

My heart was breaking for my children as well as my husband. I was overwhelmed with taking care of their needs as well as my own. I hated what this was doing to our family. In addition, I was enrolled in classes at the university and working an eight-hour day. It was not long before the stress became unbearable. I was not getting much sleep. Gabby wanted me in his presence as much as possible. Something had to give.

Finally, I dropped my class load, quit my job, and made a decision that drew a lot of criticism. I put my sons on a plane to Florida. At least I knew that they would get the attention they needed more than ever as there was just not enough of me to go around.

There were people who told me in no uncertain terms that this was not the right thing to do, but I did not get any offers from anyone to take care of them for me while I was trying to take care of my daughter and her father. It turned out to be the best decision I could have made at the time.

Gabby was livid. I did not blame him. He wanted all of his children near him all the time. He knew, however, what a strain it was for me to attend to everyone's emotional needs, as well as dealing with his relatives. At the time, I was really not concerned with his opinion or wishes. I was living this nightmare, too, and I needed to do what was in our children's best interests.

The extended-family issue I was forced to deal with in addition to Gabby's illness took a toll on my body as well as my spirit. His older sister had come out to spend time with her brother and became a stress factor for me. She found every opportunity to discourage me. She complained about everything I did. Nothing was going as she would have it. She criticized the way I managed "her brother's children." If I had not known that Gabby was still lucid enough to handle the things she would report to him during her visits to the hospital, I would have banned her from visits.

I was at a loss when I finally realized her hidden agenda. She was always looking for a way to benefit financially from every situation. And this was no different, no matter how grave and impossible. In the wake of Gabriel's lowest points during his treatment, she made constant attempts to discredit my devotion to our children. She would accuse me of neglecting them and attempted to convince him that they would be better in her care after he was gone. This was what I had to deal with in addition to the million other things on my plate. Prior to this, we had always gotten along. I loved her as a sister and thought that she felt the same. At least she behaved that way initially. Now she had become a totally different person, someone I no longer recognized.

Weeks passed, and Gabby got accustomed to the idea of speaking with his sons by telephone whenever he was up to it. His strength waned and his temperament changed. I was still angry with God. Soon Gabby was undergoing radiation and cobalt. It affected him in ways that were undeniably unfavorable, but what else were we to do? We were grasping at every straw. There were moments that I prayed for it to be over. These were the moments when he was suffering most. I asked God to stop the suffering or to please release him from his pain.

Christmas was approaching, and I begged the doctor to allow my husband to come home for awhile on Christmas Day. It would be our last Christmas together. Gabby had lost so much weight that each time I held him, I could feel his frailness. The worst was yet to come, and we both knew it.

"God, are you watching?" I asked him. "I do hope so! Just remember you are going to owe me big time for all of this!"

CHAPTER 23

Riding the Winds of the Storm

Since I grew up in South Florida, I was well acquainted with hurricane season every year, which occurred from June through November. I had weathered several hurricanes, two tornadoes, and hundreds of electrical storms. But none of this had prepared me for the storm of Gabriel's leukemia.

On the eve of Christmas 1977, as I lay awake in bed next to my husband, my mind churned with anxiety, pain, and dread for what was in store for our family. As he held me close to him, I could feel each of his ribs, because he was so thin. I understood what it cost him physically and emotionally to hold onto me. Yet I also sensed how important it was to him that I be close as he struggled to find the words to voice his thoughts. We had only one more day together at home before he had to go back to the hospital for what would be his final stay.

As he gathered the strength needed to turn my face toward him, I realized the urgency of the moment and turned my own face toward him at the exact moment that his frail fingers touched my chin.

"Little Mother," he said, using the nickname he had given me after my first visit to my obstetrician years before, "I want you to promise me something."

I sat up in bed, and drawing him close to my breast where I could cradle him more comfortably. "Okay, Hon," I answered. Not knowing what his next words would be, I prepared myself to answer as truthfully and convincingly as possible.

"You are a beautiful young woman, and I know that one day in the future, after you have been alone for awhile, you will choose to remarry."

I sat silently, so he continued. "I want you to promise me these three things: one, you will never let any man mistreat you. You have not had experience with men, as I am the first man who ever touched you physically. I love you and you are a good wife and mother. Men may try to take advantage of you; don't let them. Two, you will never change my children's names—they will remain Hunt. Three, continue to make them your first priority by taking good care of them for me. I love them more than anything, Little Mother . . . please take care of my children—promise me!"

These last two words took all of his remaining strength to utter. Perhaps this is why they became my driving force in the twenty-four years that followed.

I broke my silence and answered with conviction, "With my dying breath, I will still be keeping this promise. I love you. Remember, they are my children too."

He uttered a sigh of relief as he fell asleep in my arms.

On February 14, 1978, Valentine's Day, I made final arrangements for my husband's burial. I recalled Valentine's Day exactly nine years before when my mother-in-law was buried and the Valentine's Day twenty-eight years before when my father died, along with the deaths of others in my life which also occurred on Valentine's Day. It was a day of loves lost for me rather than loves celebrated. Gabriel knew that, and he mustered all of his strength as he struggled to hang on for me past Valentine's Day.

CHAPTER 24

What a Difference a Day Makes

That Tuesday evening, one day past Valentine's Day, I awoke from the chair I had occupied for the past two days and knew that something was different. Gabriel was no longer able to talk to me, yet we had worked out a system whereby he could use his eyes to indicate *yes* or *no* to questions asked of him. But he was restless beyond the eye movements, and I knew he couldn't hang on much longer.

I knew that the next few hours would be the most difficult ones of my life. I was grateful to God that I had at least eleven months to prepare for this day, February 15, 1978. But was I prepared? Of course not. How could I prepare for the loss of the love of my life, the father of my children, my soul mate? I knew I would lose him, but I couldn't be prepared.

As family members from far away began coming to make their last visits, I tried to get a little rest. I went next door to the family waiting area and lay down on the sofa. My heart was breaking, my spirit was defeated, my body was exhausted, and my mind was in turmoil.

My youngest brother-in-law soon came into the room to get me. "Rose, Gabby's becoming more restless. I think you should come."

I got to my feet and slowly entered the room, making my way to my husband's bedside. I met his deeply expressive eyes with my own, wordlessly conveying as much love as I could.

I placed his hands in mine. "I love you, Gabriel Hunt. I promise to meet you on the north side of the Tree of Life." He was struggling still to hold on. "It is time to let go, Honey," I quietly said to him. "It really is okay. You have fought for a very long time. You can finally be at rest." A final tear rolled from his left eye down onto his left cheek as I kissed him goodbye. And then my world crumbled. I fell into the deepest part of the abyss.

Gabriel had clung to life, for my sake, until one day past Valentine's Day. It was February 15, 1978, three months after his thirty-third birthday and exactly one month prior to my twenty-ninth birthday.

With the help of close family friends and my parents, my children and I made it through the rituals of funeral and burial.

The products of our love and devotion to each other—Ramona, age seven, Gabriel, age six, and Leonel, age five—were left without a father to nurture them. I was left with the promises I had made to care for them without him, and so my children became my lifeline.

At this point, I was not a fan of God. He and I would have to come to an understanding somewhere down the line. I was grateful that Dr. Alexander was there, and that he understood and did not judge me as did others. I knew there was no way to make sense of death to young children, so I did not even try.

I told them that Daddy had fallen asleep and only Jesus could wake him up. That did not go over too well. If Jesus was going to wake him up, they asked, " . . . then how is Daddy going to get out of the box after they put it in the ground?" This was the voice of my five-year-old, who had just had his birthday the previous November.

I tried to elaborate further. "Daddy will stay in the box in the ground until Jesus comes from heaven and wakes him up," I offered. Leonel gave me a look he still gives me this day when he can't accept my explanation for something.

I visit my life's memory banks, and they are filled with difficult days. But nothing has been as difficult as the period of my husband's illness and death. I feel, still, the joy and the sorrow of his life and his death.

Even with my strong religious background and foundation in faith, and despite my trust that the Supreme Being had a plan for my life, I could not comprehend that this was His plan. I lost my way in the year after Gabriel's death—lost it to confusion, frustration, anger, disbelief and a void in knowing no one could share my heartache, even when they tried.

My very best friend did what she could to keep me occupied. She was a constant presence, encouraging me to do things which would help in the healing process. Aunt Pauline, as the children knew her, made certain that they stayed busy. She treated them as if they were her own. She took them to Los Angeles to visit with her parents, oftentimes keeping them over the entire weekend. Geno became her shadow, even when the other two were not with them, so much so that many people believed that he was her little boy.

Yet even with help and moral support, I still felt alone and betrayed. Why would a loving God allow so much heartache and suffering? What had we done to deserve such bitter disappointment? Surely He had hidden His face from our family. Here I was, a young widow with three children, alone to face an uncertain future. What was I to do?

I found my answer in the wisdom of two very good friends. "Doc" and Velma had grown very fond of the children. We continued to be constant guests at their house for dinner, family gatherings, and simple company. I will always be grateful for their unwavering kindness, compassion, and loyalty. Without them, I would have stayed lost.

I decided to let my daughter, who was going to second grade, finish out the school year at Loma Linda Elementary. I did not want to disrupt the stability which being around her teacher and classmates would give. The boys, Gabriel and Leonel, remained with my parents in Florida while I continued with classes at Loma Linda University. It was a difficult and misunderstood decision, but I was not ready to leave what had become a comfort zone. And God and I still had some things to straighten out. My daughter and I would be away from the boys, but I was confident that I was doing what was best. Ramona proved to be the stabilizing force that got me through the rest of the semester and summer school. She became my sanity. She helped me study for my tests and final exams; she just would not let me quit.

One night, after putting Ramona down for bed, I closed my bedroom door and fell to the floor in uncontrollable sobs of grief. When I had spent myself, I stood up, gained my composure, and promised never to let grief take control of me like that again. There were things that had to be done, and crying was of no value in accomplishing them.

After taking a nice, long bubble bath, I sat on my bed. I could put off my talk with God no longer.

"Okay, God," I began. "I was taught that You always know what You are doing. Right now, I am not quite convinced that you do. Somewhere along the course of my life, You missed something. I am not sure what it is. I need to believe that you have become confused and need to regroup, so this is what I am going to do to help you with that."

I continued in earnest, "You have allowed the devil to interfere in our lives in such a traumatic way, Lord. I feel certain that he had to do a lot of talking and convincing for you to allow him to test us like this. Gabby was a good man, a wonderful father, and the love of my life. I never once heard him raise his voice or speak a word of malice against anyone."

I was not done yet. "I know that I have had my moments, Lord, when you were not pleased by things which I may have done. I asked forgiveness for them. Other than that, I have tried to be the best person I could be. I have served you all my life. I have introduced many persons to you. I have done much work in my community to help families with their children. Even now, I am still actively engaged in work at church." I was beginning to sound like the Pharisees in the Bible. "Now, I know what Nicodemus must have been feeling the night he spoke with You regarding his salvation. What have I done that you have allowed this to happen?"

It was late into the night when my conversation came to an end with this proclamation: "Thank you, God, for listening to me. I realize that You love my children and me. And since You have allowed the devil to do this evil to us, I am sure that You must have a plan of retribution and restitution. Because of this love, I know that You are going to pay me back big time. Goodnight, God, I'll talk to you later."

For the first time since that morning on a hill in Montecito Memorial Park, I slept comfortably. Ramona and I made it through! Everything would be fine.

I graduated from Loma Linda University that June. My parents came back for my graduation and brought the boys. It was so good for all of us to be together again, yet I had feelings of ambivalence as to what lay ahead for me and my children.

I sent my youngest back to Florida with his grandparents, keeping Geno and Ramona to travel by car with me. We packed after graduation and went home to Florida. Little did I know our troubles were just beginning, and that the peace I had so newly regained would prove to be as elusive as butterfly wings.

CHAPTER 25

The Games Children Play

I often hear parents say that their children constantly talk about being bored. Well, my answer for boredom is to keep children on a mission for learning. I mapped out what I would need to keep my sanity, especially with three children so close in age; it was simply three things: a sense of humor, patience, and creativity

My children were constantly learning from the moments of their births, through their toddler years, on through adolescence, and even now as adults. Why? Because their father and I taught them that learning was fun. When I was pregnant with them, I played lullabies in multiple languages, even some for which I myself had to acquire a taste. I listened to all kinds of music—gospel, country, classical, R&B, soul, and on and on. I wanted my babies to be open to it all. As they grew older, we would sing songs they learned in Sabbath School. By the time they were walking, they could recognize many tunes.

Traveling was one of the children's favorite things to do, whether by car or plane. Ramona made her first plane trip cross country when she was but four weeks old. It was a challenge to find ways to entertain them, especially when I traveled with all three by myself.

I remember one instance in particular: I was flying from California to Florida with the trio. Once I had Ramona, who was four years old at the time, settled comfortably next to her brother, Geno, I immediately told them that I needed them to play the "quiet game." They were so delighted when I informed them that there would be a surprise for the one who could remain quiet the longest. Even my youngest, who was sitting on my lap at the time, suddenly became quiet. They knew this game well. Then, soon after the plane was airborne, I told them how proud I was that they had helped me by playing the game. Geno was the declared winner. Ramona had decided that she needed the passenger across from her to answer a few key questions as the plane climbed to a cruising altitude.

When the toddlers became older and were able to speak fluently, I would have them spell simple words, at first, as we drove along in the car. It soon became a favorite pastime with Leonel, the youngest, for he could always out-spell his siblings. Leonel could soon spell anything I threw at him. I taught them phonics, and after getting beat by Leonel a few times, the older two tried to out-spell each other in an attempt to beat Leonel.

They learned to spell all sixty-six books of the Bible—and after, they learned to recite them in order both forward and backwards. Memorizing the names of all fifty states was also one of the challenges I gave them. Of course, there was always a handsome reward, like getting to choose where we would stop to eat, or perhaps the winner would get to sit next to the window for a predetermined number of miles, or maybe we would stop at the park and play for awhile before moving on. I used any motivational tactic I could think of.

The children became so adept at the games I chose for them that I was constantly thinking of new games to play. One of their favorites they played during church. With pencil and pad in hand, they would have to listen to the sermon and write down predetermined words. I would have previously written words, phrases, names of people, etc. that they would have to listen for in the minister's delivery.

At the end of church, at home, while I was preparing dinner, they would busy themselves determining who had won by having the most words. The winner would not have to participate in cleaning up after dinner. This little exercise served a twofold purpose: it kept them from distracting me during the sermon, and it made them listen to what was being said.

I instilled in the children an appreciation for learning at every opportunity. For example, they learned to identify different models of cars. And of course, if you could say it, you needed to be able to spell it. There was also the opportunity to learn math by calculating the distance between towns as we traveled from one state to the other. (Throughout their preschool years, we lived in four different states due to their father's quest for academic excellence: University of New York-Brooklyn campus; University of Miami, Florida; Andrews University, Berrien Springs, Michigan; and Loma Linda University, Loma Linda, California.)

Street names provided many hours of fascinating play. The purpose was to see how many similarities in street names occurred in different cities. There were always restaurants to name along the way, and of course, one had to spell the name of a restaurant correctly in order to eat there. Even further, a child could only have what he or she could spell without looking at the menu. It was awhile before they got to eat spaghetti. Ice cream, I think, they each learned to spell even before they learned the alphabet!

My children were quick to point out if I exceeded the speed limit at any time, so whenever we traveled for long distances, I would delegate one of them to keep me up to date whenever the posted speed limit changed; this game was quickly one I regretted inventing. But I can safely say that I was never ticketed for speeding.

Sometimes in our travels, depending on the scenery, different questions would arise. One in particular brought on a somewhat long debate among the children. Leonel wanted to know why all the black cows were grazing by themselves and all the brown cows were grazing alone in the distance. I could always depend on my youngest to get everyone's brain power going.

It was quite interesting listening to the wise one, their sister, explain this phenomenon. It made for a very interesting couple of hours and kept them occupied while I drove.

The pathfinder club to which they belonged gave them ample opportunity to test their geography, botany, and astronomy knowledge. I would have them name the constellations as well as the different kinds of plants and trees, and give some locations for each. I gained so much satisfaction from the feedback I received from my children's warehouse of knowledge. They learned and spelled all the continents and could locate the world's bodies of water before most of their peers ever heard of them.

When it came time for campouts, we all went and participated in the activities—bugs, snakes, wild animals, and all. There was no experience to compare with sleeping out in the great outdoors. Mona, Geno, and Lele enjoyed it all. This time with them was exhilarating, to say the least.

So, were they bored? No—never. The Hunt children never complained of boredom. I did not have to listen to "Are we there yet?" or "How many miles to go?" They could always figure out the answers to their own questions. And I too learned so much from my children even as I continued to find new and wholesome educational challenges for them.

Once, when I asked them to find all the names of Jesus' disciples in the New Testament of the King James Version of the Bible, my youngest became troubled by my request. Once his sister had found them all, he counted them and wanted to know why Jesus needed so many friends, especially when he had to remember all their names. So Geno (my diplomat) decided that they would each learn four names.

It served well until I asked them each to spell the names of all twelve. My youngest, who was four years old at the time, spoke with conviction when he said, "In case mommy asks me to spell all my friends' names, I am only going to have three!" He was the one to solve a problem before it even occurred.

I was faced with the same question when they were confronted with Jacob's offspring. "Mommy, I sure am glad you only had three children," was Leonel's input. But of course they had learned to spell each other's names long ago, before they knew their alphabets completely, and then they quickly learned to write each other's names.

I believed then, as I believe now, that it does not take expensive toys to make life challenging for children. Because I was forced into single parenthood at a very young age, I learned that if I could not find ways to entertain my children without spending money that I did not have, then it was my parenting skills that were lacking and not my pocketbook.

When Nintendo was introduced to the world, my children asked if they could have the game. I calmly replied that I would never buy such a toy; it was a waste of good money. They were working at the time while in high school and retorted that they would buy it for themselves. I immediately responded, "Unless you can eat it, wear it, or drive it to school, then it will never come into this house. And if someone gives one to you as a gift, we will return it and use the money for something more valuable."

They accepted my answer and never brought up the topic again. This is not to say that they never played the game. They played every opportunity they could at the neighbor's house. The neighbor's children lived in a two-parent household; my children did not. My advice to parents who find it difficult to manage more than one child at any given time is this: have fun with your children. Give them things to do which challenge their intellect as well as their physical, emotional, and spiritual well-being. Their accomplishments, as well as your own, might just surprise you.

I was labeled a "bad mother" by some of my neighbors. I was told by some of my friends that I was depriving my children of their childhoods. My children have never told me that they felt deprived, though perhaps they were deprived of many of the things I witnessed other parents providing for their children.

Perhaps I was a bit stricter in my discipline than most parents I knew. Perhaps I put too much energy into making sure that they did what they were told. Perhaps I expected more from them than other parents expected from their children.

But in the long scheme of things, my children knew, and still know, that there were (and still are) no stones that I would leave unturned for them. Perhaps this is just parenting according to me. But I am satisfied with the results of my methods.

CHAPTER 26

The PDRLs of Life

I f I thought that the devil would take a vacation from the Hunt family, I was only fooling myself. He had only just begun. We would embark upon a journey that would lead us to an entirely different and remote place in our spiritual experience. We would be tested to the very core of our existence. Ramona, Geno, Lele, and I fastened our seat belts, focused on our goals, held on tight, and settled in for the long, difficult, bumpy road that stretched out before us.

We had always had a husband and father to depend upon. What were we to do now without him? I had been introduced to death at a very early age when my father died, so I felt the loss and total bewilderment my children were now facing. It would be difficult, but we would make it. We had to persevere. I had promised!

It was time for me to have "that talk." I sat down one Sunday evening and explained to them the PDRLs of life according to Mommy: Patience, Perseverance, Discipline, Respect, Loyalty, and Love.

"In the course of your lives," I told my children, "you will come in contact with many different people with various ideas and philosophies. When you become an adult, you may decide that you want to forge your own ideas and adopt your own philosophies. But while you are under my direction and care, I will teach you what has worked for me. Your father and I believed in and lived our life together with these governing principles. Love was a given, for without love, none of these are attainable."

I can summarize the lessons I taught them as follows:

PATIENCE

Patience is the most difficult of all to learn. It must be learned first. You will be able to accomplish much more if you wait on the Lord and let Him lead you to the path He alone has chosen for your life. Many times you will be tempted to rush ahead on your own because you can see where He is leading. Never try to help the Lord out. He doesn't need our direction; we need His.

PERSEVERANCE

Perseverance breeds success. You must always keep your goals front and center of your life. *Never* give up on your goals. As long as you have breath in your body, forge ahead. You may not always be able to go at the same speed, but you must always move in the forward direction. Do not be distracted by things along the way.

The attainment of goals is like riding a bicycle. If you turn around to look behind you, even for the slightest second, you will get into trouble. You always know what you have passed in the road. You must pay attention to what is going on in front of you in order to stay on the path. Keep your eyes on the prize. Nothing can hold you back if you persevere to the end.

Sometimes I may tell you to do something, perhaps not really knowing why myself. Since I am your Mother, and you are my children, you must learn to trust that I will only do what I feel is best for you. I will be patient with you, and you will need to be patient with me. It will not happen overnight, but it will eventually happen. Just wait.

DISCIPLINE

In an attempt to learn perseverance, you must also learn discipline. Always focus on what is good and gentle in your life. This will keep you humble and grounded. When you set a goal, finish it before going on to something else. Keep your mind clear of the debris and clutter of a mundane life. Strive to always do your best in whatever you choose to do.

It is important to do your best or not attempt to do anything at all. If you think that you will fail, you will. No matter what your friends may say or do, be your own person. While those around you frolic and have fun, you will prepare to leave your footprints for others to follow.

Always remember that nothing is ever free in this world as we know it. There is a price tag on everything. You alone have the power to choose what product you will buy and how much of it.

You will have to choose the quality of your friends. You must decide whether you will follow the path of least resistance or forge your own path for others to follow. It is more expedient to lead than to follow. If you lead, you determine where and how far you will go.

You will always be in control of your destiny. Always remember to follow the first voice of your intelligence. It will never lead you wrong. Your first impression should be your only impression. It will keep you out of trouble.

RESPECT

For your sake, as well as the sake of those to whom you may be exposed, keep your distance until you are sure it is safe to venture into a friendship with them. Be respectful to all people. Allow no disrespect from man, woman, child, or beast.

Disrespect is dishonor. Do not allow dishonor to cloud your character. Give the devil no opportunity to beguile you into a false sense of entitlement. This earth belongs to God, and everything that is in it. Guard your spirit. Do not walk away if you are being disrespected. Command respect by first giving it. It will prove to be a moving force in your life. It will set boundaries for those around you. You are children of the King. Be the princes and princess that you are entitled to be. If you are faced with a choice of respect or promotion, always know that respect is the better choice.

LOYALTY

Loyalty is the greatest gift you can give to anyone. Always be loyal to each other. There is nothing that can replace the loyalty of family. If you cannot remain loyal to your brothers and sister, you will never be loyal to anyone else. Loyalty, like love, begins at home.

LOVE

Love is a vital part of everything else. It must be at the center of all you feel, say, act, and do. Love is very easy to receive, but can be difficult to give away. Therefore you must learn to love yourselves so that you will know how to love each other, and be happy to do so.

I concluded my PDRLs by saying this: "I want the three of you to know that whatever may happen in your lives, you will always be able to count on me. I may not always be right; I will surely make mistakes. But come what may, I will always defend you, protect you, support, and love you with all my heart and soul. You will always have first place in my life, after my heavenly Father."

I always gave my children the opportunity for questions. The most frequently asked was, "What does that big word really mean?" But for the most part, we each understood our responsibilities: mine was to lead the way by precept and example; theirs was to trust me to know what was best.

To a very young widow, parenting was a tremendous challenge, but I had set down the rules and was quite confident that they would serve us well. I expected bumps in our journey, but we had chosen our path and could not turn back.

PHOTO ALBUM

Mimi's Favorites

Rose Ann with her dolls; Christmas 1955

Rosalie Symonette (my Aunt Rose)

George Symonette (Daddy George)
standing; with members of his calypso band

Grandma Alice in her
favorite rocking chair

The author as
May Day Queen with
Wilbur Sims

My mother on occasion
of her 63rd birthday

Gabriel E. Hunt, Sr.
at the age of 23

Gabriel, Sr. with Geno, age 9 months; Ramona, age 24 months

Nana and Gabby (my mother and her first great grand)

Ramona, age 2;
Geno, age 9 months

Leonel, age 12 months

Geno, age 2

Geno, Ramona, Lele; the year of their Father's illness

Author's graduation
Loma Linda University

Ramona's graduation,
Loma Linda School
of Medicine

Leonel's graduation
USC School of Medicine

Geno with Gabby, age 6 mos. at his brother's graduation USC

Mother and son at his UCLA School of Medicine graduation

My Mother on her 92nd birthday

Four generations; Ramona
(holding 6 mo. old Gabby, the author; Idella, author's mom)

Nana and Gabby after
a church mission play

Ramona with Uncle Paul (the author's brother)

Dr. and Mrs. Gabriel E. Hunt, Jr. on their wedding day:
Atlantis, Paradise Island, Bahamas

Mimi's Center of the
Universe: Gabby,
Jordan, Devin

Jordan and Devin sharing

Brotherly Love;
Jordan and Devin

"Auntie Mona"
and Jordan

Geno with Jordan; welcome home kiss for Daddy

The Hunt
men with
"Papa": Geno,
Leonel, Ron
(Dina's dad)
Devin, Jordan

MIMI'S PDRLs AT WORK

Jordan with
Master Kim

Jordan with Chris

Jordan (AYSO
Soccer player)

Gabby with
her saxophone

GABRIELLE NELA'S ART

"The Violin"

"Black and White Stripes"

"Steve Jobs"

"America's Pride"

"Metamorphosis"

CHAPTER 27

Lessons in Obedience:
A Generation Removed

It was a Sunday night that put an indelible mark on the characters of my three little musketeers as they all ran around looking for their school uniforms. They always prepared themselves for school the night before. This included making sure their uniforms were ready, shoes cleaned, and so on.

I had asked them the previous night, while visiting their grandparents, to make certain that they would not forget the uniforms that I had laundered and pressed. I even went so far as to place them at the front door, but I noticed that not one had bothered to bring the items to the car as previously admonished. I drove away, knowing the tough lesson to follow.

As we arrived home and were getting out of the car, it was as if they all three had a simultaneous epiphany. I waited. I overheard, "Lele, you tell her."

My youngest replied, "Geno, you tell her."

The oldest, and self-proclaimed wisest, said, "She won't be mad at you, Lele. She never gets mad at you."

I maintained my silence.

It was not until they were ready for bed that Leonel found the courage to confront me.

"Mommy, you left our uniforms at Grammy's."

Bless his heart; he was never afraid to say anything to his Mommy, even if it resulted in severe punishment.

"Excuse me. Did I hear you say that *I* left your uniforms at your grandmother's house?" I said.

He didn't miss a beat. "You were driving the car," he said. I could always depend on this one to keep it real.

"But who was in the car with me?" I asked.

"Me and Mona, and Geno."

"And whose uniforms are they?"

He reluctantly replied, "Me and Mona's, and Geno's."

"Go get your brother and sister, and all of you meet me in the living room."

Now he was relieved to "share the wealth" with everybody. It took a moment for the clan to get an update on Lele's and my conversation, according to Lele, before they appeared. I wanted them to take responsibility for their actions, accept punishment, and suffer the consequences.

"What was the last thing I said to all of you before we left Grammy's?"

The chosen spokesperson, the youngest, said, "'Don't forget your uniforms. Put them in the car!'"

"Did everyone hear me say this?" I asked.

The middle one was now ready to contribute, "But, Mommy, you didn't say when to put them in the car. You know that you always take a long time to go when we are leaving Grammy's."

The wise one stood quietly by. He knew what was coming would not be good. The middle one continued, trying to find salvation from certain punishment.

"Mommy, we are sorry. We are so sorry, aren't we, Mona?"

Now my firstborn spoke, attempting to appeal to my inconsistencies in discipline prior to this evening.

"Mommy, can we please, *please* go back for our uniforms? We need to wear them to school tomorrow."

"I know that, darling. That is why we are all going to get them." She gave her worried brothers a look of triumph as she turned to walk away.

"I am not quite finished," I added.

She turned towards me, the triumphant look replaced with a worried one.

"You may go to bed now," I said, "because you will have to get up very, very, early in the morning. You see, you will have to walk the three miles to your grandmother's house, get dressed, and walk from there to school. I want you to always remember to do what I ask you to do and be diligent in doing so. I will not have you growing up as irresponsible adults. Not on my watch.

"And another thing: Do not ever put blame for something for which you are responsible onto anyone else, especially your mother. Do you understand what I am telling you? You each left your own uniforms. Each of you knew that you needed them. Obviously, you felt it was not a priority for you to put them in the car when I asked you to. Now we all have to suffer the consequences!"

The fog was thick with a chill in the air the next morning when I awakened everyone at 3:00 a.m. There was no complaining, no attempt to negotiate, nothing; they knew better. I backed the car out of the driveway, put them in front of me on the road, and followed as they began the long chilly, dark walk to their grandparents' house.

I could tell by the way Ramona occasionally turned her head in my direction that nothing good was being said about me. I felt so sad that they left their uniforms, but I was certain that after this episode, it would not happen again.

After the first mile, we had reached an intersection. I stopped and let them get into the car. They were cold and defeated but said nothing as I crossed the highway and once again stopped the car to let them out. Then the tears began.

"Mommy, we won't ever do this again. Please let us get in the car for the rest of the way." Geno made the case for everybody.

"I am sorry, son. I cannot go back on my word. Actions have reactions and consequences. You must learn this. If you learn nothing else in life, you must learn this! So get out of the car; you still have a ways to go."

Ramona seethed as she opened the door and slammed it shut. *That child has a lot to learn about discipline,* I thought. She was going to be my cross.

Upon our return to the house, their grandparents were in frenzy. "You should not do this to these children," they said. "This is no way to raise children. They are cold and tired."

"Well, you know what?" I asked. "So am I. Children must learn obedience without question. They must learn to respect what parents say and do. My children will learn that consequences for their actions will not always be easy to bear. So the next time they are tempted to wait until a more convenient time to do something I ask them to do, they will think twice about not doing it right away.

"I may not have this parenting thing down just right," I continued. "But I know that there are three of them and only one of me, and I refuse to fail at disciplining them when they can learn the lessons necessary to make it in this world."

No one said anything more to me after that declaration. I allowed my dad to take the kids to school, only because they needed to eat breakfast, and I needed to get back home to get ready for my work day. I know that my children remember what I taught them. We talk about their life-lessons still and laugh—now that it is their turn to become parents themselves, and they understand what I tried to accomplish.

The boys were much easier to discipline than my sweet, beautiful little girl. She was more willing to test the waters of my discipline than her younger brothers. I am sure it was the family's fault that she had this false sense of entitlement. We all spoiled her. I was raised as an only female child. She was the only girl child in the family. She received so much attention from her grandparents that she thought that she was the only child in the universe.

Her father had adored his little "Monz," as he affectionately called her. All little girls have that special place in their father's heart, I think. I know that my Daddy Ray loved and adored me. And Ramona's brothers asked for her opinion on almost everything! No wonder she felt that the world was her oyster. I had to bring her down to reality in a hurry.

A few years had passed since the uniform incident. I had asked my daughter to wash her sneakers over the weekend so they would be dried by Monday. Needless to say, this had not happened. So she waited until she was getting ready for bed that night before remembering she did not have clean sneakers for school.

She also knew that I did not believe that nasty sneakers were attractive, no matter what other parents believed. I did not care that it was not cool to have clean sneakers. My children were not going anywhere in filthy clothing, and that included shoes.

Anyway, she hurriedly washed the sneakers before going to bed. The next morning, she put them in a hot oven to dry. In her constant haste, as she dressed for school, she forgot the sneakers. I knew that they were in the oven much too long but kept my silence.

When she did remember, the sneakers were burned and stiff. When she left for school, I asked why she was not wearing her sneakers. She told me that she decided to wear other shoes.

Well, I knew that she had physical education class and volleyball practice. She was not getting off this easy!

"Go get those sneakers, and put them on," I ordered.

Ramona was not pleased with that order and gave me a look that she will live to repeat only once in her lifetime.

"Mommy, I can't wear those to school. Can I please just take them? I will wear them for P.E."

"No, Ramona, you will wear them all day, and if I come to the school at any time today, and they are not on your feet, you will not want to know what your punishment will be."

My face was so familiar on my children's school campus, I was often taken for one of the instructors, so Ramona knew that she could get caught quite easily at any moment during the day. She was not going to take the chance. My children never knew when I would spend my lunch break at their school, just checking up on what was going on; occasionally, I would take a personal day off just to walk around campus. I needed to know what was going on at their school.

I attended every sports game in which they were involved, whether it was basketball, baseball, football, volleyball, or softball. They participated as players; I participated as a parent. I have sat in the pouring rain until 3:00 a.m. at baseball tournaments. I have cheered at softball competitions until my voice became hoarse. I have driven thousands of miles following the teams on which my children played. I have yelled at opposing teams not to hurt my sons on the football field, much to their embarrassment. And, yes, I was threatened by the umpires with putting me out of the park. My lips were sealed against my will on many occasions.

I was my children's most ardent, dependable, enthusiastic cheerleader. All the referees got to know me personally. There was always one of the Hunt children playing something, all throughout the year, even Little League and city league baseball. I was always asked to cease coaching from the bench, but I knew it was harmless.

My parents would attend all of the Little League games that they could; they went on out-of-town trips; they would enhance the cheering section. They wore the team colors, shirts identifying them as Geno and Lele's Gramps and Grammy, respectively. My children always had loving grand-parents to dote on them.

When they became teenagers, I often thought that if my mind was not already gone, surely I would lose it now. I neglected to have foresight enough to remember that having a kid every year for three straight years would mean that one day I would have three teenagers all at once.

In my defense, I surely did not anticipate having to deal with them without their father. Grandparents, I soon learned, were not meant to discipline, especially not teenagers. It was always, "Wait until your mother finds out." I doled out all punishment, so I became the bad guy. On occasion, my mother would greet me with, "Here comes the joy killer!"

God knows those teenage years were some of the most difficult times of my life—not that discipline was a big problem; it wasn't. My teenagers thought that I was certifiably insane; they still think so. My motto was and continues to be, "Whatever it takes!"

My offspring learned very early that I believed in action and reaction. They could always tell the severity of the punishment by the definition of the crime. Sure, they tested my boundaries, but they never knew what I would do at any given time. For instance, once I took Geno out of a baseball game to do the dishes he had neglected to put in the dishwasher.

Ramona saved herself from many a punishment by escaping to her grandmother's house, once she was driving her own car. Leonel was saved on several occasions because he would let me know exactly what had happened, even when he knew that he would be punished. Honesty worked wonders for him, though his brother and sister were not happy about this.

CHAPTER 28

Hard Lessons Easily Learned

Growing up in a religious family instilled many wonderful qualities within my character. I have appreciated those precepts. I held onto them with fervent hope and tenacity. I lived according to the Ten Commandments of God's law as taught by the church.

I was a firm believer in chastity and the sanctity of the human body. I believed so much in what I was taught that no one and nothing could dissuade me. I took my chasteness to my marriage bed and belonged to one man only until death separated us. This I have never regretted, for it was the right thing to do.

I was quite satisfied with my beliefs and my church until the day my youngest son was left at the altar for the third time, after requesting baptism. It was then that I took a new look at my church and its principles—written and unwritten.

Lele had witnessed the baptism of his siblings the previous year and now wanted to take this most important step. So he had made his wishes known to the pastor of the church and had stood up front with other prospective members, as the custom was. He remained as each of the other participants was greeted, hands shaken, etc.

After everyone had gone back to their respective seats, he alone stood at the altar, ignored by the minister and elders, until I finally went forward to get him. This sequence of events occurred again twice after the first episode. It became obvious to me that the pastor was deliberately ignoring my child.

I was not going to let this man disappoint Lele any longer, so I solicited the cooperation of the pastor of my parents' church. After all, the only thing my son wanted was to be baptized. The pastor of my parents' church, where I had grown up, told me, "You and your children are not members of my congregation, so I cannot baptize your son."

But I thought that we had to go through baptism in order to become church members. Maybe the rules had changed, and nobody had informed me. I still do not understand the reply the pastor gave me. I became so frustrated with the whole thing that I told my son that I would baptize him and left the whole issue alone. The devil was really trying me, and I needed to regroup in order to prepare for what was coming next.

I had taken employment at the parochial school run by the "sister church" in order to relieve some of the burden of private school tuition for three children. As an instructor, I would receive a ten percent discount on tuition. This is why I found myself constantly making excuses for the behavior of certain church members who ran the school. It escaped them that a young widow with three very young children might need some emotional support. Little did they know that I was now hanging on to my childhood beliefs by a thread. It never occurred to any of them to ask how I was really doing. If they cared, I missed the concern.

For the most part, the school board tolerated me. I was the ticket to their school's secondary accreditation. As long as I performed according to their plan, everything was good. I watched the other teachers in the school very carefully and learned a lot through my observations.

It was at the end of my first year (after accreditation of course) that I suddenly discovered how unhappy everyone was with my performance. Two sisters who were at best barely-average students (and also identical twins) failed two of my courses. I was asked to change their grades to reflect passing scores. Clearly I had made a mistake, according to the principal.

When I refused to bend to such tactics, my children became victims of passive-aggressive actions. When the school board realized that I had done nothing wrong and that they could not legitimately fire me, they asked me to resign. When I refused and said they would have to fire me, the real war began.

Because I had refused to do something as unethical as passing students who had failed miserably despite my efforts to help them, my children were punished.

I was informed on the first day of school, in August of 1982, that my children would not be allowed to stay in school unless the full tuition for the entire school year for the three of them was paid in full. Just imagine the impact of that for a single parent with three children attending private school! I asked other parents if this had ever been required of them, and of course it had not.

Nevertheless, I had made some promises that I was not going to break, and so I submitted the check for the full amount to the principal. I will never forget the look on his face as he made sure of the correct amount. Then, to add insult to injury, I was informed that all the milk money had to be paid. This was a bit much for me to handle all at once, and I was close to tears, but held back. I would never let them see any sign of weakness coming from me.

I refused to dance to that tune, so my children were banished from the school. My youngest was dragged outside still sitting in his chair because he refused to get up from the desk. He was nine years old! This was the very same child who would later be left standing at the church altar by the minister. Subsequently, I led my heartbroken children away from the parking lot, determined in my heart that on this day, I would find a school that would take them if it were the last thing I did.

There was another private school quite close by, so it was my first stop. The children waited as I went into the front office and made inquiry of any openings. The principal was a very warm, caring, and sympathetic individual who informed me that, yes, indeed there were three openings at the school. I could not contain my exuberance. "The students," he continued, "will have to take an entrance examination, and the school board will have to make the final decision based on set criteria."

Since school had already been in session for two weeks, we would be late, and he was concerned about scheduling the tests as soon as possible. I told him my children were outside in the car and could take the tests right then. The principal was concerned they would not do well, given their experience just half an hour earlier.

The fee, of course would have to be paid for the exams, along with the first month's tuition and registration fees for each child. I took a much-needed deep breath, asked the Lord to please intervene, and I suggested he begin the testing while I secured the funds. The principal, seeing how determined I was to get my children into school, acquiesced.

Away I went as my children were left in a school office filled with strangers, their faces streaked with dried tears, to write the entrance exams. I gave them my regular pep talk, (trying to convince myself more than cheer them up) that everything would be fine.

Upon my return, I found them still testing, so I took the opportunity to speak more frankly with the principal. He informed me that the students presently enrolled at the school were all Caucasian, and he was not sure how this would affect my children. I reassured him that my children would not be adversely affected, as they were the only black children initially enrolled at their previous school.

By this time, the testing was completed, and the children returned to me. The look of utter relief on their little faces made my heart glad. They felt that they would be in school soon. They knew that they had done well on the exams. They always did well. We left the school quite light of heart.

It turned out the school board was scheduled to meet that very night, so we would most definitely be in school the following day. It was so wonderful to hear my children speak of their "new school," even though they were going to miss their old classmates and friends.

But then there was the problem of school clothes. They wore uniforms at the old school. I couldn't believe God had brought us this far to leave us now. Oh, yes, we would sleep well tonight! That was our plan. God's plan was quite different, we would soon learn.

As promised, bright and early the following morning, we all traveled to what promised to be the "new school." There was never a question as to what the test scores would reveal, even under stress brought on by extenuating circumstances. The principal called me aside as we entered the office.

"I have some news for you," he began. "You have brilliant children. Their test scores are phenomenal. They never missed any answers and tested way above their grade levels; as a matter of fact, they tested above two grade levels each. They would be an asset to any school which they attend."

I was very pleased to hear this, but he was not telling me anything I did not already know. So my question to him was, "May they visit their classrooms now?" We were all four very anxious, and I still had huge dragons to slay over at their last school.

I felt that I had been hit by a Mack truck at his reply: "I am afraid to tell you that the board voted against them."

When I regained my composure, I asked, quite perplexed, "Why?"

"Well, the board members were afraid of the reaction from parents of the enrolled students to the presence of black children attending school with their white children."

"This is 1982," I offered in return.

The principal's answer came back with additional poison. "I am so very sorry, but you may not be refunded your monies for the testing. A portion of the tuition will be reimbursed." I had paid part in cash, part by check.

This would be the second-most difficult thing I would have to tell my children, second only to having to telling them that their father was going to die.

The disappointment on their faces revealed the ache in their hearts. They cried uncontrollably as the non-baptized one, my youngest, lashed out at me for taking him from his beloved school. He was nine years old at the time and had decided that it was entirely my fault. I could not argue with him, for all I had needed to do was change a few grades for two red-headed twin girls.

Why should I care whether the girls knew that they did not earn the higher grades? After all, in the words of the principal of Sampson School, "They are never going any further in their education after high school anyway." (I don't know after all these years if he was right or not, but it does not matter. What does matter is that my children are all educated.)

I stopped the car abruptly. I turned toward my son in the back seat, as my daughter in the front seat watched me with fear in her eyes. She realized that her little brother had almost committed the unpardonable sin by the tone in which he had addressed me. I said a quick, silent prayer as I voiced a promise to the trio.

"James E. Sampson Memorial School does not want you in their school any longer, and I will put you in public school before I would ever consider sending you back there again. And I promise you that come Monday morning, with God as my witness, you will be enrolled in school. I promise you this!"

It was a long, silent ride back to their grandparents' house. I needed to be alone to plan my next strategy. I had just made a promise which I had no idea how to keep.

Back in my car alone now, my tears and sobs came in such a torrent that I had to pull over to the side of the road to regain my composure. Questions flooded my mind. Did I make a drastic mistake in bringing my children back to this dreaded place?

My daughter had been enrolled in first grade already before we left California. She loved her school and the teachers. How could I do this to her? I was certain she would never, ever forgive me. Her brother, my oldest son, had been in pre-kindergarten and loved every moment of it. His teachers adored him, and there were many playmates. I wondered what he could be thinking now, and whether he would someday forgive me.

Then there was my baby, the youngest, who never understood why Daddy was always throwing up and then had to go in that big, brown box in the ground. He was in love with his teacher at the preschool in Loma Linda. I knew in my heart that even if he would tell me someday that he forgave me, he could never understand how his mommy could allow this to happen. I felt at this moment that I had become the least-liked person in their lives.

What awful thing had I done to my children? As I asked myself these questions, I reached down to retrieve the tissue that had fallen to the floor of the car. I dried my tear-drenched face and glanced in the rearview mirror, where a sign appeared to read Palm Vista Church of God School K-12.

I turned my car in the direction of the driveway, drove up to the door marked "Office," and got out. "Dear Lord," I prayed, "let them have room. Let them accept my babies."

When I entered the office, the principal happened to greet me. Right away, I felt at peace, and a wave of relief passed through me as he shook my hand and introduced himself. I explained that I wished to enroll my children in school and told him of the disappointment we had encountered earlier.

As he listened, appalled but with interest, he inquired as to the grade levels of the children. There apparently was no room in their respective grades. Since the children had already taken entrance exams from the other school, that would prove sufficient for Palm Vista. I would, however, have to obtain the records from Sampson for each child.

I happily registered each of them for school. I actually sang as I recorded the information necessary on the applications. God really was still on His throne, I mused. In any event, my children would be able to start school the following Monday. I was more than ecstatic.

My next step would be to secure the school records from Sampson. All I needed to do was drive over and pick them up. So with much trepidation in my heart for having to go back to that place, I pulled into the yard and exited my car. I spoke with the "loving" principal and requested the records.

No, I would not be given the records, he replied, nor would he send them to the school. I promptly informed him that yes, indeed, the records would make it to Palm Vista if I had to call the sheriff to get them, which is what I did. But to my knowledge, Palm Vista was never made privy to those school records. I cannot be sure, but I still wonder.

When I informed Palm Vista's principal of what took place, his question still makes me ashamed when I consider it: "And these people call themselves Christians? Bring your children in on Monday, and we will do the rest. The scores from IRA will suffice for now."

Needless to say, my children thrived at Palm Vista. They were involved in extracurricular activities at the school as well as in the community. Ramona played volleyball and softball and became quite good in both sports. The boys played baseball and basketball at school and with the city league. Their trophies fill a case I still display.

CHAPTER 29

Faith as a Grain of Mustard Seed

Despite our recent victory, I knew that my faith was faltering. I felt alone and abandoned. Again I asked, "God, are you still here? Why does everything have to be so difficult?"

His answer was sure: "I am always here, and you are never alone!"

One summer day began with my youngest pleading with me to attend a youth meeting held in Miami, Florida. I had traveled the night before with my parents and the children, who were now all teenagers, to the site of the meeting. Little did I know that my life would take a surprisingly abrupt turn.

I had no plans to expose myself to the hundreds of people who were gathering to hear the speaker for the morning service. But after much pleading and compliments about my hair and clothing from my children, I decided to attend. I really did not want to disappoint them. I convinced my family that I would follow them as soon as I finished dressing.

I made certain that I took my time in getting to the convention hall, secretly hoping that I would not be able to find my family in the crowd and that they were not successful in saving a seat for me. When I reached the auditorium, I reluctantly opened the door. The ushers told me that finding a seat would be a challenge. I looked around for a split second, took in the massive audience, and had turned to leave when I spotted my family down front. Why on earth would they sit right in the middle of the aisle, four rows from the stage?

By the time I made my way down to where they were seated, I realized that the speaker was someone from my past. I had not seen him since my last year at college. The Lord was still leading. There was a transformation in my life that day that I have not spoken of until now. I will not ever forget the sermon or the man God used to deliver it! It took me back to an evening at Oakwood College, in Huntsville, Alabama.

During my freshman year, I was standing on the steps of Cunningham Hall, chatting with friends. A young man approached, asking to have a moment of my time. He was not just any young man. I had secretly hoped that one day I would have an opportunity to speak with him. He was an upperclassman, and I had been boosting my courage to approach him.

I had watched him from afar as he worked around campus. I was especially drawn to the sound of his voice. And now, as he stood at the bottom of the steps, his eyes searching my face, I was at a loss for words. His eyes were kind, his lips moving nervously as he asked me for a date.

I had already made plans for the evening in question with my room-mates. I could have kicked myself as I looked into those questioning eyes of his and replied that I had previous plans. My mother had taught me never to break a promise.

He walked away without another word. I knew that there would be plenty of time for me to go out with him. I hoped that he would ask again, but he never did. I was very disappointed later to learn that he had become involved with someone else.

I continued to watch him from afar as he moved around campus. Even after I became involved with the love of my life, and got engaged, I wondered why that young man never asked a second time for a date.

I finally learned the answer to my twenty-one-year-old question as we had an opportunity to talk that afternoon. He had not taken my refusal well. He had taken my response as total rejection and had feared the same fate if he asked again. Once that issue was cleared up, we talked at length about our families, mutual friends, and life in general.

I opened up to him as I had not done with anyone since I became a widow some eight years prior. It was such a relief to get it all out. He had no idea that he saved me from myself that day. I still thank him at every opportunity for reminding me that God only wants what is best for my children and me. It was such a relief to pour out my soul to someone who cared.

It caught us both by surprise when we discovered that we had been on the same campus for two years at Andrews University in Berrien Springs, Michigan, and never came in contact with each other. My third child was born at Berrien General Hospital. I was thrilled to learn that he had married a camp-meeting friend of mine.

I made him promise to keep in touch. I needed his wisdom and spiritual leadership. I promised to keep the faith and continue to trust God, and I endeavor to keep that promise. The bond of our friendship and mutual respect, co-mingled with our love for God, continues. He keeps me grounded; I keep him accountable to our friendship. His deep love for his Master and dedication to serving Him inspires me. His abiding respect for all that is right and good challenges me to be the best that I can.

I left south Florida the next morning, renewed and refreshed. I was so happy that God had worked His mysterious magic. Whenever I pause to reflect upon His blessings, I count my beloved friend as one of God's greatest gifts to me. I am sure that my children noticed the remarkable influence he has had on my life.

CHAPTER 30

Change and Challenging Times

It was a great adjustment for the three Hunt children as they entered public school for the first time. Ramona was the first to go in her sophomore year; Geno and Lele entered the year after. Private school classes had been much smaller, and there were fewer teachers and much smaller campuses. I prayed that they would make the transition smoothly. I had to make quite an adjustment in my disciplinary techniques. This was a whole new ball game for me too.

The kids got involved in sports right away. The boys had participated in Little League baseball and Geno had played basketball and baseball in junior high, so it was only right that they continue. Ramona joined the volleyball team. She became quite good at the game, and her fierce serves resulted in many points for the team.

I always motivated my children to strive to become the best at whatever the task. This lesson proved to be a problem for them as they endeavored to make new friends and acquiesce to the varied teaching methods of public school teachers. They were very good students and were not popular with certain classmates who were not as gifted intellectually.

The Hunt children, as they were referred to, were honor-roll students, members of the yearbook staff, *Who's Who Among High School Students* nationwide, and players on the football, baseball, and volleyball teams. They also each had part-time jobs after school and on weekends. The youngest held down three jobs at once during one semester and made the honor roll every grading period!

In other words, their self-esteem was always intact. They inherited genetically favorable looks, so they were often picked on by jealous classmates. They dressed well and were always well-groomed and well-mannered. Sometimes they suffered the consequences of good behavior.

One night, after a victorious football game, my sons went to a post-game hangout to get a bite to eat. While chatting with some friends, Geno was approached by another teenager; he brandished a gun.

The boy made the accusation that Geno was interfering with his relationship with a particular girl and threatened to shoot him if he did not stop trying to take his "woman" away from him. I am more than sure that this was a very scary moment for Geno, his brothers, and their friends.

To make matters scarier, Geno had no idea what the boy was talking about. He seldom had any contact with the girl in question. He was a very well-known and liked football star, and this was often trouble in the making. He simply could not be a good student, good-looking, the best area-wide receiver, and a more than decent baseball player and not have trouble come his way. When I learned about the incident later that evening, I was livid. Furthermore, I didn't think highly of the girl in question, and that insulted me further.

I visited the principal's office when the first opportunity presented itself to see what could be done about the threat. My son had already taken care of the matter before I arrived. It was then necessary for me to speak with the parents of the girl in question, so I made a telephone call before visiting them and explained to the grandmother that I had no intention of having my son involved in altercations brought on as a result of their child spreading rumors. I was incensed, and they knew it. That was the end of that!

It was difficult raising teenagers in my hometown. The area was infested with drugs. There were dealers all around who were constantly being arrested and then put back on the streets; there were high school bullies ready to threaten and endanger. But I ruled with an iron fist and a lot of discipline and love—and above all else, I had steady conversations with God.

My teenagers were, all in all, good teenagers, though not without the normal testing of boundaries and pushing a few curfew rules. I put the fear of God and Mother Rose in them early on in their training, and I stayed on my knees in supplication to God for guidance in rearing them.

Their grandmother was often their saving grace when punishment was dished out. Ramona would always threaten to go to Grammy's when she was displeased with me. My answer to those threats was, "If you go, don't come back." Much as she loved her Grammy, a daily dose of being at her house was not as appealing as she pretended. I needed her to know that I was the one in charge of her character molding. It was my responsibility to make certain that she obeyed the rules in my house so that it would become natural to obey, wherever she happened to be.

There were things that my teenagers did that they still have no idea that I knew. This was intentional. At some point in a child's life, he must learn to let his conscience be his guide. The funny thing about a conscience is that it will keep you humble. So even though I sometimes worried silently, I knew for a fact that they were suffering enough for the questionable deeds.

Graduation day was fast approaching for my daughter. She had been accepted at a number of colleges, had made *Who's Who Among American High School Students*, was on the yearbook staff, belonged to the high school chorus and National Honor Society, and so on.

CHAPTER 31

Things are Not Always
What they May Seem

On the eve of Ramona's graduation, my stepfather summoned me to his living room to discuss a matter with me. He and my mother had decided that, in his words, "You do not need to worry about Ramona's schooling. We will take care of it for you."

"What does this mean exactly?" I asked.

"Her four years of college will be taken care of so you can concentrate on getting the boys through high school."

I could not believe my ears. I wondered why my mother was not in on the conversation at the time. In fact, she never spoke to me directly about this plan. During the ten years that brought us to graduation, neither of them had ever made mention of such a gift before, and I was shocked beyond words. With a grateful heart, I accepted and offered my thanks. I could now concentrate on preparing the other two for graduation in a couple of years.

Being the now "independent black woman" which the death of their father had made me, I had already prepared for Ramona's entrance into the University of South Florida. She had been accepted; financial aid forms were filed (despite the promise made by my parents), student loan applications were submitted, and all was well. She was not yet seventeen years of age, and I welcomed the close proximity to home that the University of South Florida afforded.

The ultimate goal was for her to attend the alma mater of her parents, Loma Linda University, by way of Andrews University, Berrien Springs, Michigan. Ramona's grandparents had discussed with her the possibility of attending the school in Alabama from which her father graduated with his baccalaureate degree, the school where her parents had met and fallen in love twenty years before. But Gabriel and I had decided long before Ramona was conceived that this school would not be an option for our future offspring.

Her grandparents were not pleased with this decision and made their feelings known, but I stood my ground. It was not their decision to make, and I truly believed a sixteen-year-old young lady should not be so far from home.

In preparation for the inevitable disappointment that I felt was forthcoming, Ramona took the navy admission exam. Afterward, she received an appointment for her physical down in Miami at the naval recruitment center. I was not happy about any of this but had to have a plan B. It became the most beneficial avenue at the time.

The whole time that she was in with the doctor, I prayed that God would intervene if this were not the route we should take. I was very nervous when the door finally opened and the doctor stepped out to talk with me.

"I think your daughter will serve well in the United States Navy," he said, very pleased with himself.

"So she passed the physical?" I asked.

"Except for one minor problem, which we can fix, with your permission," was his answer.

Ramona had problems with her shoulder when she played volleyball, but I was not willing to let her go through unnecessary surgery just to serve in the navy. And there had not been any indication that the surgery would be the last one she may have to endure. She didn't mind. But she was still a sixteen-year-old minor who needed my permission. We needed guaranteed financial help for college, but not at that price!

I told the physician that we would get back to him, and we left. Ramona was not happy, but I did not concern myself; she would have to get over it. The Lord would provide. He always does.

CHAPTER 32

Dealing with Broken Promises

I t was in the very early morning of the trip to Tampa for pre-registration that I first learned the meaning of some words I had found inscribed on a piece of plywood in a religious bookstore:

> *Once upon a time, when life was like a gentle rhyme, I thought God's gifts were free for the asking. Now it's another time. I've found few things to be as I thought they would be, but I have found that God's gifts really are free for the asking.*
>
> *—Unknown origin.*

I see those words even now when I look up from this writing pad.

All packed up and ready to say goodbye, my daughter and I stood at the door of my parents' home and waited for them to come from their bedroom to see us off. When no one came forward, I went back to inquire as to the check for the registration. I am convinced that my stepfather thought he was doing something great when he retorted, "I am not paying for her to go to no heathen school!"

The words tore through me like a two-edged sword. I had used what monies were left to purchase dormitory essentials, etc., believing that I did not have to worry about tuition. It was now 3:00 a.m. At this hour, what was I to do? I pleaded with him to lend us the money. I would pay him back.

He was unforgiving and said, "Not unless she goes to the church school."

I had no desire to fight with him or plead my case any longer. "Very well," I said. "We will see you when we get back."

I had no idea that the promised payment of college expenses had strings attached. It had always been a given to have prayer before anyone went on a long trip away from home, so we waited for the invitation to pray, as always from Ramona's grandfather, but it never came. He was only in the mood for prayer when he had his way and was in control. We prayed for ourselves, knowing God always answers my prayers.

I had learned previously that what my stepfather said he would do and what he planned to do were not always one and the same, and my mother was consistently silent. It was my job to be confrontational. With that in mind, I had not wholeheartedly trusted her husband's words of promise to pay for Ramona's schooling and had sent in all the required financial aid forms. However, this did not solve my immediate problem.

I have had a few people on whom I depend when I have needed help, and it was one of these dear friends to whom I now turned. He came through with the necessary funds for my daughter and drove over with us to Tampa to get her registered for school. He will never understand the extent of my gratitude. I am eternally grateful. No matter what I asked of him, he was always very willing to help me where my children were concerned, even when I didn't ask.

I cannot go on here with Ramona's story without being reminded of other influential people in our lives. In particular, this chain of events took me back to the kind, loving, and compassionate influences of the parents of one of my childhood friends. Mom Hall and Mr. Hall, as I addressed them, were always ready to listen to me and lend their advice. Without passing judgment, they would lend an ear as I questioned my lot in life.

They were also constant influences in the lives of my children. My oldest son swears to this day that Mom Hall could make the best grilled-cheese sandwiches in the world, and she was always willing to make them for him! He felt so special at those times. The Hall house became a place of refuge for me as well as my children on so many occasions.

I constantly reminded my offspring that people would judge them by the company they kept. I also shared one of my mother's best adages: "Water seeks its own level." I wanted to make certain that they chose their friends carefully, and the boys did. They were well known by many, but only a chosen few enjoyed the privilege of really knowing them. I was adamant about that.

Arie Joseph became like a third son to me as the development of a most profound and gratifying friendship evolved with Geno and Lele. He played ball throughout high school with my sons. He was much taller and more developed in stature than both my sons, so he took it upon himself to be a surrogate guardian of sorts.

I was never concerned about my boys' safety as long as Arie was with them. And whenever I missed them, I knew they could be found at the Fague household. Arie's mom, Marie, and her husband, Michael, still serve as surrogate parents. This couple opened their home to my children as if they were their own. The camaraderie, love, and influence for everything good continue to this day. Geno, Lele, and Arie grew up together and enjoy the fruit of their friendship some two decades later.

They became so close that whenever Geno and Lele were punished, Arie shared in the punishment. I adopted him long ago as a "third son," and I treated him as such. He was reprimanded whenever I felt it was needed. He was always respectful, kind, and grateful for any advice I would give.

These boys continue to look out for each other. That's what good friends do. I am forever grateful that Arie came into our lives.

During this time, I became more closely acquainted with the mother of a friend to Leonel. It is my ardent belief that God brings certain people into our lives at the time in which they will play the most important part and give us the most blessings. This friend did just that.

Johnnie and I were brought together at this point in our lives to the greater good. We had matriculated at the same high school and were already acquainted. She stepped in just in time to help my youngest son and I make it through some of the most challenging times of our lives.

Johnnie's son, Ronald, and Leonel were the best of friends. They were together like brothers once Geno and Arie left for college. They would hang out at both houses. When we couldn't find either of them, we knew that wherever they were, they would be together, so we did not worry too much.

Leonel loved hanging out at Ms. Johnnie's because she was such a good cook, and he loved to eat. He would never go hungry at her house! She loved to feed him and loved making people feel comfortable and at home. I will never be able to repay her for the kindness, love, and devotion she exhibits to this day to me and to my family. We soon became the rock to go to for each other whenever there was trouble brewing in our camps. Parenting was all-consuming in our lives. We wanted our boys to come out on top. We laughed and we cried. We had occasional differences in opinion but always respected each other's point of view. She is still a one-in-a-million friend.

The boys felt they were our protectors. They would sometimes attempt to tell us where we could and could not go. I remember one time in particular during the rival game of the year for two colleges which would take place in Tampa, Florida. Our sons had already made plans to attend. We, the moms, had discussed going along. This was not met with approval by our teenagers. "You two will not be going to the game," they warned. We replied that we could go where we wanted but agreed that they would not have to sit near us, or even see us for that matter. We would drive our separate vehicles.

At last, though, we relinquished the idea of going, which made the boys happy, and they left the following day for their planned weekend. Johnnie and I decided to stay at home and entertain ourselves as we often did, just relaxing and doing chores.

But as we talked and reminisced about parenting, we made the decision that we would indeed go to the game that very afternoon. So we gassed up the vehicle, went to the mall for outfits, and had something to eat. I believe that we were attempting to gather enough courage and energy for the long trip to Tampa. We would show those sons of ours who were in charge! We drove to the stadium and bought tickets at the gate, making certain to sit on the opposite side from where we knew the boys would be sitting. It rained the entire game, and when all was said and done, we had sat through the downpour, become soaked, and had no changes of clothing. Afterward, we made the trip in the thunderstorm across the treacherous Highway 60 back to our homes. Our sons still do not believe we attended that game.

CHAPTER 33

Meeting Challenges Head-on

The first year of my daughter's college education was one of many changes for us. It was during this time that I learned what she had decided would become her ultimate goal. She had been so very talented in the humanities that I was certain that a career in journalism or art was in her future.

To my amazement, she informed me that she would follow along the path begun by her father—medicine. My greatest concern was how to encourage her to do something for which we had no financial backing. But nonetheless, I knew that I had a promise to keep, and I was determined to do just that. And so the next three years were spent finding ways to keep her on the path she had chosen.

After Ramona's first full year at the University of South Florida in Tampa, I felt she was now mature enough and experienced with the college routine sufficiently. So with an ambivalent heart, I sent her off to Loma Linda University.

Even though she was now enrolled in a "church school" and my step-father decided that now he could feel good about "helping," I was still reluctant to trust him. I was in a state of constant unrest. Every year I would fill out the financial aid applications to ensure that she would still be able to attend school if at any time he stopped contributing. This made his contribution much less than he had declared he and my mother would pay. Ramona also took out student government loans. I made sure to remind her that she could only count on her mother and herself one hundred percent; any other help was just a luxury.

Ramona worked throughout her undergraduate program and during the summer in order to graduate on time with her class. I constantly praised my Heavenly Father for His intervention. I was able to secure scholarship monies to relieve some of the burden of student loans. Were it not for perseverance, determination, strength of character, and God's leading, Ramona could not have fulfilled her dream of graduating college. But she was now ready for medical school.

God intervened, and I learned of a civic-sponsored scholarship that would provide financial relief. That scholarship, along with government loans, made it all possible. A secretary, Ila, where I was employed, informed me about this scholarship. I applied for my daughter, and she was awarded $60,000 for her four years of medical school. I am so grateful for Ila's suggestion.

With Ramona in college, I had more time to devote to my sons. Along with their academic achievements, part-time jobs and athletics, the boys were well-liked by their classmates and their teachers. However, popularity bred a whole new set of problems, especially for my oldest son. Because he had his father's charm and good looks, the girls all liked him. He was kind, compassionate, smart, a football hero, and he owned a pair of girl-melting light-brown eyes. Geno spent his senior year with a fair amount of girl trouble that continued for many years, but as with all challenges he faced, this too helped make him the strong, courageous young man he is today.

Geno was a very accomplished baseball and football player and turned down numerous athletic scholarships in order to attend his parents' alma mater. But after high school graduation, off he went, his hand in a cast due to a broken wrist suffered during practice in the football season. I was so happy that I finally had sent another child off into the big world of college academia. He would join his sister at Loma Linda before transferring to UCLA. The same scholarship which his sister was awarded became salvation for him; he was awarded $15,000 yearly for four years. Each year we had to apply all over again, but it was well worth the effort. And then, of course, government loans, grants, financial aid, and work-study programs all helped him get through his chosen program.

The nest indeed was soon to be emptied of fledglings, and my baby boy and I were left alone to face the world. It was now his senior year in high school, and some year it was. As I watched him grow into a very mature, wise, young man, I felt more blessed than ever to be his mother.

Leonel had determined very early that he would earn a scholarship to attend college. True to his word, he was courted by such schools as University of Florida, Princeton University, University of Miami, Duke University, and John Hopkins, to name only a few. He had already decided that he would obtain a biomedical engineering degree before going on to medical school. As he confided to me one day, "If my sister and brother can decide to do medicine, so will I."

Johns Hopkins University won out over the other schools. He passed inspection by the alumni who interviewed him and was accepted for the fall term into the engineering program. This program, I later learned to my chagrin, would take five years to complete.

The thought of having all three children in college at once was frightening enough. But an added year made me feel faint. How would we ever get through it? Johns Hopkins came through for my 4.3 GPA student with a full tuition scholarship. And yet again, the Fort Pierce Memorial Scholarship Fund awarded Leonel $15,000 yearly as long as he kept his grades up. Yes, God still reigned supreme, and off Leonel went to Baltimore, Maryland.

As I look back on those college years for my three children, I realize that each one of them has his or her own story to tell, and I hope that one day they will tell of their struggles, their victories won, and their battles lost.

Because the scholarship to Johns Hopkins only lasted for four years and his program of study was five years, my baby decided that it must only take him four years to get his biomedical engineering degree. And he did the almost impossible; fours years it was.

Consequently, in June 1991, June 1993, and June 1994, our family traveled first to Loma Linda, California, then back again, and finally to Baltimore, Maryland, for college graduations.

The days at Johns Hopkins were difficult for Leonel because this was the first time in his life that he was all alone without any family near him. His first major accomplishment was battling the bitter cold of his first winter in Baltimore. He was not prepared for it. He had lived in California and then Florida prior to encountering a Maryland winter. At home, my heart was heavy as I spoke with him at least three times a week. But he was my Hopkins son, and I was so very proud of him.

Leonel made sure to leave his mark at not only the university, but also the Baltimore community. He was instrumental in starting a mentoring program for inner city boys and spent many hours involved there. He worked with a neighborhood "Heart, Body, & Soul" health program and received a commendation from the Governor of Maryland for his efforts. He devoted countless hours in helping prepare flyers, pamphlets, etc., when his fraternity sponsored a cotillion to raise money for victims infected with the AIDS virus, and he spent significant time at the hospital counseling. Those times I would speak with him by phone and hear the true satisfaction in his voice, I was that much more proud of him.

Sometimes during the course of any single parent's life, I am certain the same questions I asked myself were being asked by other parents. Am

I doing the very best that I can for my child? Can I do more? Should I do anything differently?

One night, Leonel called me, sick with the flu virus; he said, "Mom, I am so sick." I wondered, *Did I do the right thing in sending him off to Baltimore?* But during our conversation, he told me of an experience he'd had that week which inspired him. Upon hearing this, I knew I had done the right thing. When he called at yet another time to let me hear how disappointed he had been to earn a "C" grade on an examination because he was involved in other extracurricular activities, I forcefully reminded him that this was not acceptable because he was at Hopkins; he was first to maintain his academic standing with everything else following in second place. Once again, I wondered, *Should I have done anything differently?*

I was given my answer when he called with the news of another exam on which he had excelled. When I occasionally stop to peruse the many plaques on the family room wall which pay tribute to the accomplishments of this Hopkins boy, I know for sure that I did the only right thing!

Meanwhile, out west, Leonel's siblings made their individual marks on the campus of Loma Linda University and University of California Los Angeles. Ramona and Geno were both engaged in research and had been named when their work was recognized in the *American Journal of Medicine*.

I have many opportunities to ponder the accomplishments of these three remarkable children. When I remember the trials, temptations, and tribulations which they endured to become who they are today, I marvel at the reality of it all. Am I the woman who brought them into the world? Is it I who was allowed the privilege of rearing them? Am I really their mother?

What is it about little, insignificant me that I was given the wonderful gift of knowing these three magnificent human beings? They are not only kind, loving, and compassionate souls, but they have not given me one moment of heartache. When I think of all of these things, the answer comes back: "You are not an ordinary woman. You are a most blessed woman!"

During Ramona's matriculation in California, she busied herself with her academic studies but found some time to sing with the gospel group well known as "Another Peace." She has an appreciated alto voice and used it in bringing sunshine through music to the lives of others.

As I sat listening to her in concert, I was so proud of the young woman she had become. She was personable, witty, extroverted, kind, and yes, even if I say so, simply beautiful. She was born beautiful. Her father had emphasized this at every opportunity afforded him.

CHAPTER 34

Making Good on Promises

The very first college graduation was Ramona's, and we all antici-
pated it. Leonel traveled from Baltimore, and I and her grandparents from Florida. We were ecstatic as our first college graduate made her
way across the podium to receive her diploma. Another milestone had been
reached, with many more to come.

Ramona had been accepted to the fall entering class of 1995 at Loma
Linda University School of Medicine. The summer would be spent preparing for this next step. There was much work to be done. Medical school
would present a whole new range of mountains to climb. But I knew God
was still in control and had it all planned. No worries! One step at a time.

Next came Geno's graduation from UCLA. I had been in an unfortunate automobile accident and had experienced serious back surgery just
three months prior to graduation day. I was unable to climb steps and so
had to slowly, painstakingly, take the long way around, across the Bruins
Football stadium where graduation services were held. Yet the pain I experienced that day simply melted away as my second child walked across the
podium and accepted his diploma. Thank you, God, for blessing me.

My oldest son would enter medical school at UCLA in the fall. What were these children of mine trying to do to me? I would have two children in medical school at once. Was I up to the challenge? Oh, yes, I was! God and I had an understanding. He would not have brought us this far to turn His back on us now. Of that I was certain. At least these two children would be in the same state with only an hour's driving distance between them. I was grateful.

More than one person has questioned me upon occasion as to which of my children is the special one. My answer prior to now had always been the same: Each child has something unique that makes him or her extra special to me.

Contrary to that feeling right now is that of the uniqueness of my baby boy, and I trust that when my children read this they will understand and appreciate what I am saying.

It was graduation day at Johns Hopkins University, June 1994 instead of 1995. This lone fact, in and of itself, made this day extremely special. My youngest child, my baby, received his biomedical engineering degree one year earlier than the class with which he began. So as I watched him walk across the stage, hand outstretched to receive his diploma, I felt an overwhelming degree of freedom as well as pride.

My mind raced back to a delivery room twenty-one years before in Berrien General Hospital, Berrien Springs, Michigan. It was some minutes before midnight as I lay on a delivery table feeling content and satisfied with no sense of the real urgency to expel a child from my womb.

I had been in labor for an appreciable length of time and was at a point where the child would not come. He was lodged in my pelvis and was soon to be in distress. I remember the doctor urging me to push, but I had no desire, no strength. I only wanted to sleep.

It was when I heard a nurse ask if she should get the mask that I realized something was definitely wrong, and so at his last demand that I push, I felt my husband's hand support my shoulder as I attempted to lean forward. As I gathered one last ounce of strength, the future biomedical engineer entered the world.

He was met with numerous sighs of relief and appreciation, accompanied with total shock from his mother. I wanted to know if the wrinkled, yellowish, scrawny package really belonged to me. It was not until the next day that I learned that one of us was not expected to make it through this delivery.

Thank you God, for blessing me. This child, who was scheduled to arrive on February 14, 1973, had just made his appearance on November 30, 1972. This child who was supposed to be delivered by Dr. Gerald Relkin at Mercy Hospital in Miami, Florida was just delivered by an aspiring orthopedic surgeon in Berrien Springs, Michigan.

And this all happened during the worst blizzard recorded in thirty-three years. The significance of the events of his birth, the gift of life for him and I both, were never more apparent than some twenty-eight years later as, surrounded by his equally accomplished brother and sister and his loving grandparents, I watched him receive his degree. *All things work together for good to them that love God.*

CHAPTER 35

Continuing Promises Kept

In August 1991, we began yet another journey when my daughter, who applied to a grand total of one medical school, began with the entering class of 1995. She had even applied for early decision. This child had inherited her mother's unmitigated gall, but best of all, she had faith in her abilities coupled with complete faith in the God who had created her. She had no doubt that she would be a member of that class.

Leonel had accomplished the goal of getting into medical school with a flourish as well; he had been accepted to the University of Southern California Medical School. So off he went to California to join his siblings.

I would now have three children enrolled in medical school, three thousand miles away from home. They were all now, at least, in the same state. The boys were in Los Angeles, their sister in Loma Linda.

Geno and Leonel, although attending different schools, were able to live together and share expenses. Leonel's full tuition scholarship at University of Southern California Medical eased much of the burden and stress financially. He was the one child who had informed his family years ago that we would not have to worry about his school tuition, and true to form, he was right.

Whenever I extract scenes from my memory bank, each graduation stands out above all other memories—first high school, then college, and most vividly of all, medical school. I think about the years of struggling to overcome financial burdens, and I realize how miraculously we were led to accomplish it all.

I remember the nights I lay awake wondering where the next dollar would come from to help pay rent, buy food, clothing, furniture, books, and on and on. Those years were the most challenging of my life. Of course, there were doting grandparents and friends who helped along the way, but ultimately the responsibility was mine and mine alone. There were people who would say, "Girl, you have nothing to worry about; you have parents to support your children's education."

I will never minimize the part my parents were willing to play in helping me with the children, but even gifts had their price. I felt I was ridiculed and reprimanded if I chose not to follow the rules according to my parents' way of thinking. And the church, rather than being a source of strength, only added to my disappointment and frustration. On one specific occasion, when all the children were home on vacation, I asked them to attend their grandparents' church. We were all sitting together when a church member coughed up a most vile mouth of mucus and spat it onto my youngest son's neck.

The spittle ran down the back of his neck to the collar of his shirt before I could get tissue to catch it. I was livid. I bade them to arise from their seats. We left, and neither Leonel nor his brother has ever returned to that church. They were now adults and could make their own decisions about church and religion. I never forced them. They each have their own relationship with God, as do I. It is unfortunate that it does not include attending Macedonia SDA church. I knew there were many other churches that would welcome us, and though it was not a popular decision with my stepfather, we never felt we could return. My stepfather merely made excuses for what happened, stating that his "church people" could do no wrong. Neither could he.

Choosing the directions I felt best was not always without a price to pay. I kept in mind the morning of Ramona's registration her first year of college, which would always serve to bring me back to reality when I had the need to ask for assistance. Whenever I found myself desperate to come up with emergency funds for the children, I would ask everyone else first, afraid to resort to family for help since the church was held over my head as a bargaining tool.

If, after much third-degree questioning, I was given the help requested, it would more often be followed by, "Will you be going to church this week?" or "I will buy you a dress for your birthday, but only if you are going to wear it to church," or "No, you may not use my car on Friday night; I don't know where someone will see my car parked." I quickly came to realize that, according to their philosophy, all I needed to do to find favor and have a life free of stress and worry was to be in church every time the door was opened. It did not seem to matter what was gong on inside of me as long as on the outside I was not making any waves.

There were so many moments when I began to feel so terribly alone in the struggle. There were moments when I became so emotionally, physically, and spiritually exhausted that I questioned the practicality of what I had promised to do so many years before.

The most amazing thing of all is that from the night in that hospital room at Loma Linda University Medical Center, February 15, 1978 to the present, the only people who have asked *me* how I was doing have been these three children of mine and three very good friends. It is not that I did not feel that people cared. It was just nice to hear every once in a while, "Rose, how are *you* doing?" or "What can I do to make this easier for *you*?"

If it were not for the encouraging words during long talks and moral support by dear and loving friends, I would not have had the strength to continue on my spiritual journey. Unlike family members, these friends did not judge me, but accepted me as I am. They did not care whether I went to church or not. I had not missed one week of attending church in all my life until the birth of my first child. I had experienced my own workable relationship with God for a long time. My friends were aware of this, and I was very grateful.

My sons, I know, are especially grateful to the two men who have encouraged and stood by them in times of faltering faith and disappointments brought on by hard trials. These men were always there to lend a hand, whatever the need. Role models were very few, and these two gentlemen filled the void with nothing asked for in return. Their spiritual, emotional, and physical gifts will never be forgotten.

CHAPTER 36

Almost Journey's End

It was once again graduation day at Loma Linda University Medical School, class of 1995. I sat in anticipation as my firstborn stood to walk across the stage to receive her diploma. The person directly in front of her made his way. Then "Dr. Ramona Raymonde Hunt" echoed in my ear. For a few moments my world stood still.

I felt a lump in my throat as I held back the tears. "Well, Gabby," I whispered, "one down, two to go." It was a moment which I could not ever describe to anyone in words. Dr. Hunt—this was my baby girl, my beautiful Dr. Hunt. I think how she would have made her father so very proud, were he here today. I felt a chill run through my body before at that thought; perhaps he could see her after all.

That same evening, our family made our way to the church where her wedding would take place. This was rehearsal for the big day. I experienced a myriad of emotions at this time but could not discern an apparent reason. Somehow I had to shake the feelings before the next day. I was not pleased by the choice my daughter had made, but it was her decision, not mine, to make.

There was something about this young man that puzzled me. I couldn't put my finger on it just then, but there was something. Even then, I did not trust him. Little did I know that the years ahead would reveal the reasons to me. Of course, I always want what is best for all my children, and it was apparent to me that this was not what was best for my daughter.

I sat in my place on the first pew and watched with anxiety and anticipation as she walked down the aisle on the arm of her grandfather. I had made an early morning visit to Montecito Memorial Park to visit Gabby's grave site, and despite my earlier composure, I was, at present, heavy of heart. I was also very angry.

The anger I felt brought me back to a place where I had no desire to be right then. I did not have time for the feelings; I needed to put them on the back burner and stay in the present. Yet I could not shake the feelings, and I let them wash over me like an enormous wave rushing me toward a churning ocean.

The coffers of my memory bank again overflowed with every step that I had taken to that point. I was filled with such overwhelming emotion. There was no turning back now, so I tried to ride the wave back to solid shore, though it did not happen quickly.

My daughter was much closer to me now, floating down the aisle, dressed like a princess. Oh, how very beautiful this child had grown up to be. She looked like an angel as she walked past my pew.

My heart felt as if it would explode with the wealth of emotions. It was if I had just watched her through two pairs of eyes. And as that horrible feeling of emptiness washed over me, I began to sob uncontrollably.

As to those around me, I am sure only a select few could feel and understand my pain. It became increasingly difficult to regain my composure as I sat and listened to the ceremony.

All the years of her life which brought us to this point moved slowly across my mind: her very first piano recital, her gymnastic competitions, her flute lessons, her first game-point serve on the volleyball team, the first person she threw out as a catcher on her high school softball team, her first days in the dormitory at USF, her first job in high school at McDonald's, the fights we had as mother and daughter. I knew my tears were because I loved her so dearly. I had been given the privilege of sharing all of these milestones, but her father had not. I was angry because he was not here. I was angry because I wanted him here.

It was at this instant that I realized a profound fact: I had not ever really taken time out to grieve his absence. I never had time because I had made a promise, and I had to get busy keeping it. I realized that day, on our first-born's wedding day, how much I missed him and how sorry I was for the things he could not share.

And as I gazed through my tears at my two handsome sons standing on the podium with their sister, the realization that I must go through these same feelings twice more was more than I could bear. Yet when my quick-thinking youngest son came down to console me, I managed to compose myself long enough to hear the remainder of the wedding vows. The feelings that came up that day took a few years to resolve, but at least I was able to get through it.

Ramona chose to embark upon a career in family medicine which took her to a program in Orlando, Florida. Two years later, I found myself in the observation room watching my first grandchild make her appearance into the world.

She was the most magnificent Christmas present her mother could have given me. Little Gabrielle tugs at my heartstrings like no one else can. She inherited her Grandpa Gabby's eyes. God, once again, smiled on me. Each moment I get to spend with her is special. I count her as one of my greatest joys.

CHAPTER 37

Continuing Milestone

The University of Southern California presented its graduating medical class of 1998. The graduates had already marched in; my parents and I, along with little Gabby, had been caught in traffic and missed the processional. Nonetheless, my son was seated where we could easily find him in the crowd. There was a sea of crimson gowns across the auditorium's floor level.

We cautiously made our way upstairs to the balcony as it was now time for the diplomas. I pinched myself as I thought, *And to think I get to do this all over again in a couple of weeks*. My mind played terrible tricks on me as I sat in the balcony waiting to hear his name called.

I heard his sister say, "My little brother is an M.D. No way!" Funny, I thought; she was only two years older than he and she was an M.D. The announcer called his name: "Dr. Leonel Alexandre Hunt."

"That's my son," I yelled. "That's my baby boy!"

I am sure he heard me and may have felt a teeny bit embarrassed. I didn't know and did not care. He had to be used to my methods of showing my pride in him by now.

"Well, Gabby, two down, and one to go," I whispered. "I told you that I would keep that promise. The boy really does look good in that cap and gown. The crimson made him appear more handsome than ever. We did good! Yes, we did!"

Watching Leonel interact with his niece after graduation was over made me realize how wonderful I felt to have been afforded the opportunity to mother this gentle, loving, intelligent human being. I am truly blessed. I actually felt a little guilty about being so very blessed. I was walking on air and I think everyone around me could tell.

The Surgeon General of the United States was the commencement speaker for the UCLA College of Medicine, Class of 1998. I was becoming a real pro at this graduation business, but this one was different in a way I could not fully comprehend until I found myself analyzing the event much later. My oldest son, born twelve hours before his father's twenty-seventh birthday, had become a medical doctor. Dr. Gabriel Eugene Hunt, Jr. had a very significant ring to it as I heard them calling him forward.

I felt certain that my heart would burst with the pride and the joy I experienced as I watched him walk across the stage to receive his diploma. Life could not get much better than this. This middle child had endured so much to achieve his goals, yet through it all, he persevered. The stumbling blocks became footstools to a greater service. The disappointments were lessons in forbearance. The emotional upheavals were tests of faith. And what a stalwart, self-assured young man he had become.

I was finally free! I had kept my promise as best I could. The children I had vowed to take care of would now be able to take care of not only themselves, but also scores of others. The joy I felt was inexplicable. I wrote the final chapter of this first book in my mind on that day.

As I watched Geno interacting with his niece, I mused to myself, *Gabby, we did it. You and I have given to the world the best that we could—three wonderful, magnificent human beings.*

When I had time alone that evening to reflect on the past three weeks of my stay in California, I gave thanks to the most Sovereign Being for what He had done for me and the fruit of my womb.

I felt so very special to have been afforded this great privilege to have been influential in the lives of three people who would serve humanity in such a capacity. I felt most honored to have them call me "Mommy." And I know that the lives of those patients who are touched by these three great physicians will be blessed—first by the warm, tender, compassionate, loving spirit of Ramona in her role as corporate physician for Rosen Hotels in Orlando, Florida; secondly, by the strong yet gentle and sincere caring of Gabriel Jr., neurosurgeon, as he makes the quality of life better for his patients as director of Spinal Cord Injury at Cedars-Sinai Hospital, Los Angeles, California; and lastly, by the steady, sympathetic, nurturing attitude of Leonel in his orthopedic spinal surgery practice as director of Cedars-Sinai Spine Trauma Center. One does not operate without the other assisting.

If perchance humanity is affected half as much as my life has been blessed in nurturing these wonderful children, then all will be well, and I will truly be free. It still boggles my mind. My license plate, MOM3MD, is always there to remind me, but occasionally I catch myself shaking my head in amazement at the wonder of it all.

CHAPTER 38

Fulfilling the Legacy

As the Hunt physicians settled into their chosen specialties, I experienced new-found vigor and vitality in my role as their supportive and loving mother, as well as a grandparent to little Gabrielle. She was growing up so very fast, and I wanted to be ever-present for her entrance into the realities of life. Gabby was a constant delight to me as well as my mother. Her uncles seemed to watch her in amazement each time they saw her. I secretly thought it was as if they were in disbelief that their big sister was now a mother herself.

When I was forced into a very early retirement due to complications from back surgery, I was elated to spend more quality time with my granddaughter. It was such a thrilling and adventurous period; I basked in the joy of taking an active part in rearing the first child of the next generation. There was no end to the fascination of watching Gabrielle grow and learn.

By the time she began her entrance into formal academia, I was convinced that she would be a most precious and productive gift to the world. She was already playing the violin as she entered first grade. It was a rare treat to hear and absorb her through the music emitting from her violin as she ran her fingers along the strings.

Gabby excelled in whatever she engaged in. She excelled in gymnastics, taking home many awards by the time she was seven years of age. I am proud to say I made certain I was present for each milestone. We became a likely twosome wherever we went, and developed a bond that exists now.

Because Gabby had the distinct pleasure, as did her mother before her, of becoming the very first grandchild and great-grand child, she was lavished with all the love, attention, and time that any child could have from everyone in her family. Each of us, without shame or guilt, showered her with everything imaginable. She wanted for nothing.

Her uncles adored and doted on their niece and wasted no time or expense in making her feel their love and affection. They were both still single, and therefore had no children of their own. But all that would change. It would take eleven long years, but someone else would come along to share in the dynamics of grand-parenting. And so the legacy will continue.

CHAPTER 39

Friday the Thirteenth

On Friday, April 13, 2007, my family was thrust into yet another role as we mourned the loss of our reigning matriarch, my mother. "Grammy" as her grandchildren called her, and "Nana" as affectionately named by her great-grandchild, left us early that day as we watched her life slip away and out of our reach. We had enjoyed her leadership as the loving, devoted mother and grandmother all of our lives; now we were at a loss as to what we would possibly do without her.

As I held her cooling body in my arms, singing the very first song she taught me as a child, I recalled the anonymous quote I found engraved on that piece of mahogany years prior, and it comforted me. I had pressed my lips against the pulse in her neck, and when I felt it fall eerily still, the memory continued to sustain me:

There have been times in my life when I thought that God's gifts were free for the asking. Now it is another time. I found few things to be as I thought that they would be; but I have found that God's gifts truly are still free for the asking.

My grandmother, Alice, was the first person I remember saying that a rainbow always comes after the storm. Well, this storm was over. The rainbow would soon appear, and I was totally ready.

Three months after my mother's demise, Gabriel Jr. was married on Paradise Island, Bahamas, the country of my birth. And though it was a bittersweet time, this union would bring much joy and happiness to our family. As my older son repeated his vows, I secretly ventured back in time to another time, another place, when his father and I promised ourselves to each other. Gabriel Sr. would be so proud and happy with this union. I still miss him.

My mother had the privilege of meeting her grandson's choice of a soul mate and voiced to me how much she thought of Dina. She was happy that her "Geno" had found such a "good girl" with whom to share his life. This wedding was one of the times that I missed my mother most. My new daughter-in-law would prove that my son had indeed found his "pearl of greatest price". She was everything that a mother could ask for her son. I love her as if I gave birth to her, and I have since become as a surrogate mom. Dina lost her mom prior to her marriage to Geno, so I am honored to have this relationship with her.

Near the end of summer the following year, I became a grandmother for the second time. Little Jordan Gabriel made his entrance into our lives on August 18, 2008. It was the day after what would have been the thirty-ninth wedding anniversary of his grandfather and me. These bittersweet moments continue to come to me.

When I looked into that beautiful fresh face, so full of promise for the future, I felt so much love and adoration that I feared my lungs would explode, my heart would stop beating, and I would surely stop breathing. And when I finally held him in my arms, I knew in my heart and soul that he had now taken his place along with Gabby amongst my heartstrings. I would never be the same again.

CHAPTER 40

A New Generation

The move to California was inevitable. I packed up most of my possessions during Dina's pregnancy and moved out to California the week prior to Jordan's birth. I did not intend to miss out on one single moment of my first grandson's beginning of life out of the womb. I also knew his parents could benefit from any help I was willing to give them. I have never regretted the decision to relocate.

Leonel, my younger son, made the move stress- and finance-free. I was also more than pleased to finally get to spend some quality time with my sons for a change. They were involved in their practices and making their marks in the medical arena. And as I watched them use their talents to improve the plight of healthcare for individuals within their care, my heart would fill to overflowing with pride in each accomplishment.

To my delight, our growing family welcomed Devin Alexandre to the fold almost two years after his big brother. Now that my older son had sons of his own, I was now in the proverbial "fifth heaven". Being a grandmother is everything I imagined it would be.

There is no greater satisfaction than watching my offspring reproduce and contribute to the world. I give thanks every day for my family.

The business of being "Mimi"—as I came to be known by my darling grandchildren ("Grandma" had no special appeal)—held me within its spell. But it did not, however, dissipate the yearning I had to interact with Ramona and Gabby. I missed them terribly. They were now settled in Orlando, Florida where Ramona serves as director of Functional Medicine at Rosen Medical Center. We spend major holidays together and keep in touch on a daily basis via the modern technology at our disposal. Gabby spends school break in California with the rest of us. She and her little cousins enjoy a mutual attraction and appreciation for each other, and are always ecstatic to spend time together.

Ramona, meanwhile, does all within her power to keep her father's legacy alive. In addition to her work at Rosen Medical Center, she joins her siblings by lending her medical talents and expertise to the people who may benefit from her dedication to making healthcare available to those who are deprived of the necessities of proper health care.

As for me, I look forward to the time when I may once more welcome a new offspring into the world. I exhibit all six facets of "The PDRLs of life".

When I reflect on what might have been, had the love of my life been afforded the pleasure and pain of watching our children grow and mature into the fantastic human beings they have become, or when I revel in the intense joy and satisfaction of playing and interacting with our grandchildren, I am stunned into the reality that I am more than truly blessed.

The author with her grandchildren; Devin, Gabby, Jordan

UPDATE

The Hunt Foundation

When an earthquake ravaged Haiti in 2010, many thousands of citizens of the Republic were left destitute and homeless. The desperate population reeled with the devastation and ruin of their homeland as they pondered what to do next.

It was not long before the airplanes began landing with survival supplies: food, clothing, fresh water, and blankets. But most importantly, there were medical supplies brought by medical personnel. Doctors, nurses, volunteers from around the globe all made the sacrifice to come to the aid of their fellow men and women at a time of great peril.

Doctors Gabriel E. Hunt, Jr. and his brother, Leonel A. Hunt, desired to lend a helping hand in any way possible as a neurosurgeon and spine surgeon, respectively. When met head-on by political ramifications and bureaucratic red tape, they refused to become discouraged; instead, they decided to form their own foundation in order to make a difference in their own way. Subsequently, "The Hunt Foundation" came into existence.

Since its inception, The Hunt Foundation has been instrumental in taking teams of medical personnel to Gabon, as well as Ethiopia, on the continent of Africa. Their team has performed life-altering and life-saving surgeries on the citizens who came in need of their services.

Dr. Ramona Hunt, the family practitioner in the group, saw as many as one hundred patients each day of the week when she joined the group in Gabon. Ramona was no stranger to mission trips around the world; she had spent two weeks in Jamaica caring for children riddled with disease during her residency, and administered to approximately eighty patients each day while on a mission trip to Nigeria. She is a valuable member of the team.

Meet the doctors:
(L-R) Leonel A. Hunt, M.D., Orthopedic Spine Surgeon;
Ramona R. Hunt, M.D. Family Physician;
Gabriel E. Hunt, Jr., M.D., Neurosurgeon

THE HUNT FOUNDATION AT WORK
IN ADDIS ABABA, ETHIOPIA

The Hunt Foundation;
Trip to Ethiopia welcomed by the children

The Hunt Foundation Info Board

Waste Water Treatment Plant in progress

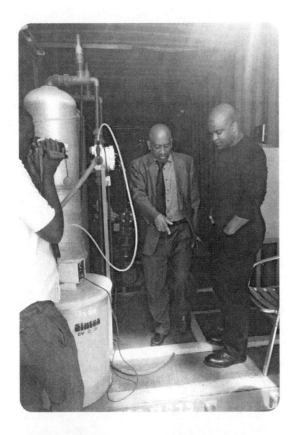

Dr. Gabriel Hunt, Jr. inspecting the Waste Water Treatment facility

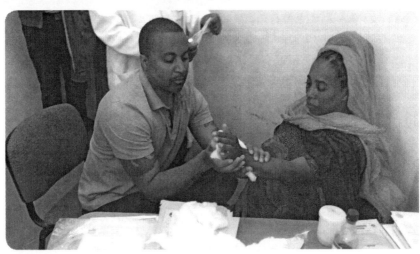

Dr. Leonel Hunt, orthopedic surgeon, with a patient

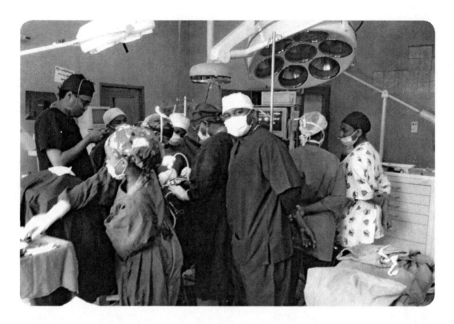

Dr. Gabriel Hunt, Jr. (facing forward) observing surgery

Dr. Leonel Hunt (L), Dr. Asfaw Yigeremy and Dr. Gabriel Hunt, Jr. (R) pose in front of Hunts Neuroscience Center

About the Author

Born on Long Island, Bahamas, Rose Hunt is the loving mother of two sons and one daughter, and the devoted grandmother of three grandchildren. Her passion is and always has been for family; her greatest joy comes from making a difference in the lives of children whenever and however the opportunity presents itself. Through the strength of her upbringing and by virtue of her challenges as a widowed mother, she crafted a set of parenting principles called "The PDRLs of Life", specifically built upon the values of patience, perseverance, discipline, respect, loyalty, and love. Using this approach, she worked hard through the child-raising years and celebrates the positive outcome as exemplified by the many successes of her children. To this day, she follows these same principles as she commits her life to being the best mother, grandmother, and friend possible.

ACKNOWLEDGEMENTS

With significant thanks:

To Gabrielle Nela, my beautiful, smart, and talented granddaughter for allowing me the use of her artwork.

To Claudia E. Hughes, my beloved and trusting friend for taking on the task of reading the very first draft of my manuscript. Without your diligence and hard work in attentiveness to each word I wrote, and advise and opinions, this may not yet have been a reality.

To Robert E. Brown, my most precious friend, for always being there for me and my children. Without your willingness to help in whatever form, I most certainly would not have made it through some of the most difficult times of our lives. You never judged me. You gave of your time, your listening ear, your advice and expertise without asking for anything in return. Our friendship spans more than half a century, and I am eternally grateful that the bond we share is an unbreakable one. My children and I thank you.

To Ila Lecato, a friend who cared enough to point me in the right direction. Without the Fort Pierce Memorial Scholarship Fund, my children's reality may have been much different.

To my children, Gabriel, Ramona, and Leonel, the driving force behind everything that I have done and will continue to do, for your support, love and understanding. Thank you for trusting me enough with your lives to follow my PDRLs, and for helping to make MOM3MD a reality. I love you!

To my FriesenPress family for your enthusiasm and positivity toward my project.

To all of you, my friends and acquaintances for encouraging me to "write a book" after hearing my story.

CPSIA information can be obtained
at www.ICGtesting.com
Printed in the USA
FSOW02n0116300117
30176FS